The Arno Press Cinema Program

CLOZENTROPY
A Technique for Studying Audience Response to Films

F. Dennis Lynch

ARNO PRESS
A New York Times Company
New York • 1978

Wingate College Library

079836

This volume was selected for the
Dissertations on Film Series
of the ARNO PRESS CINEMA PROGRAM
by Garth S. Jowett, University of Windsor, Canada

Editorial Supervision: Maria Casale

First publication 1978 by Arno Press Inc.

Copyright © 1972 by F. Dennis Lynch

THE ARNO PRESS CINEMA PROGRAM
For complete listing of cinema titles see last pages

Manufactured in the United States of America

Library of Congress Cataloging in Publication Data

Lynch, Francis Dennis.
   Clozentropy : a technique for studying audience response to films.

   (Dissertations on film series) (The Arno Press cinema program)
   Originally presented as the author's thesis, University of Iowa, 1972.
    Bibliography: p.
    1. Moving-picture audiences. I. Title.
II. Series. III. Series: The Arno Press cinema program.
PN1995.9.A8L95   1978   301.16'2   77-22911
ISBN 0-405-10754-4

CLOZENTROPY: A TECHNIQUE FOR STUDYING

AUDIENCE RESPONSE TO FILMS

by

F. Dennis Lynch

A thesis submitted in partial fulfillment of the
requirements for the degree of Doctor of Philosophy
in the Department of Speech and Dramatic Art
in the Graduate College of
The University of Iowa

May, 1972

Thesis Supervisor: Professor Samuel L. Becker

FOR BARB, MIKE, AND PENNY

ACKNOWLEDGMENTS

I would like to thank my fellow graduate students at the Television Center of the University of Iowa, and my colleagues in the University Film Association and on the faculty of the University of Kansas School of Journalism, for their many helpful criticisms and their willingness to serve as guinea pigs. My mentor for the past decade has been Sam Becker, and I owe him special thanks for his continuing encouragement. The idea that made this thesis possible was suggested by Professor Don Darnell of the University of Colorado. The program for the cloze data was written by C. J. Bangert of the University of Kansas Computation Center (it was my good fortune that he was a film buff and able to make many valuable theoretical suggestions). Bill Maxwell, Jim Frane, and Pete Klammer also provided invaluable help with the computer and the analysis of the data. John and Mary Bremner provided useful editorial criticism. And I don't think this dissertation would exist at all if it hadn't been for Ab Schulman. Thanks to you all.

TABLE OF CONTENTS

Page

LIST OF TABLES ....

LIST OF FIGURES ....

CHAPTER
- I. INTRODUCTORY DISCUSSION 1
  - Experimental Research in Film 2
  - Information Theory and Audience Response 4
  - Clozentropy 8
  - Design of This Research 15
- II. PRETESTS 17
  - Design of the Stimulus 18
  - Design of the Response Instrument 20
  - Subjects; Test Procedures 25
  - Explanation of Clozentropy Data 26
  - Results and Discussion 32
  - The Problem with "Gunsmoke" 41
- III. THE CLOZENTROPY INSTRUMENT 43
  - Restatement of the Problem 44
  - Redesign of the Stimuli 49
  - Redesign of the Response Instrument 51
  - Subjects; Test Procedures 54
  - Results and Discussion 55

CHAPTER		Page
IV.	SUMMARY AND CONCLUSIONS	73
	Summary	74
	Conclusions	74
	Suggestions for Further Research	76

BIBLIOGRAPHY		82
APPENDIX A.	LIST OF INTERRUPTIONS IN PHOEBE AND HOW DO I LOVE THEE	86
APPENDIX B.	PRETEST QUESTIONNAIRE	89
APPENDIX C.	MAIN TEST QUESTIONNAIRE	105
APPENDIX D.	SAMPLE OF RESULTS FROM MAIN TEST	123

LIST OF TABLES

Table		Page
1.	EXAMPLE: COUNTS OF RESPONSES	27
2.	EXAMPLE: PROBABILITIES	27
3.	EXAMPLE: ENTROPY	28
4.	EXAMPLE: RELATIVE ENTROPY	28
5.	EXAMPLE: INFORMATION/RESPONSE/BLANK	29
6.	EXAMPLE: ABNORMALITY	30
7.	EXAMPLE: SUBJECT ABNORMALITY	31
8.	MEAN NUMBER OF CORRECT RESPONSES (29 POSSIBLE)	36
9.	CORRECT RESPONSES, FIRST AND LAST THIRDS	37
10.	MEAN NUMBER OF CORRECT RESPONSES SOPHISTICATED/NAIVE SUBJECTS SIMPLE/COMPLEX ITEMS, PRETEST DATA	39
11.	FINAL TEST RELIABILITIES	55
12.	MEAN RELATIVE ENTROPY SCORES	56
13.	SUMMARY TABLE, ANALYSIS OF VARIANCE, MEAN RELATIVE ENTROPY SCORES	58
14.	MRE SCORES, FILMS-BY-LEVELS COMPARISON	58
15.	MEAN NUMBER OF CORRECT RESPONSES AND VARIANCES	68
16.	SUMMARY TABLE, ANALYSIS OF VARIANCE, NUMBER OF CORRECT RESPONSES	69
17.	MEAN NUMBER OF CORRECT RESPONSES, FILMS-BY-LEVELS COMPARISON	70

LIST OF FIGURES

Figure		Page
1.	RELATIVE ENTROPY, PHOEBE, FIRST CUT	34
2.	SUB-GROUP COMPARISONS, ENTROPY, PHOEBE, FIRST CUT	34
3.	PLOT-SHOT ENTROPY COMPARISONS PHOEBE, SOPHISTICATED AUDIENCE	60
4.	PLOT-SHOT ENTROPY COMPARISONS PHOEBE, NAIVE AUDIENCE	60
5.	PLOT-SHOT ENTROPY COMPARISONS LOVE THEE, SOPHISTICATED AUDIENCE	61
6.	PLOT-SHOT ENTROPY COMPARISONS LOVE THEE, NAIVE AUDIENCE	61
7.	SOPHISTICATED-NAIVE ENTROPY COMPARISONS PHOEBE, PLOT LEVEL	63
8.	SOPHISTICATED-NAIVE ENTROPY COMPARISONS PHOEBE, SHOT LEVEL	63
9.	SOPHISTICATED-NAIVE ENTROPY COMPARISONS LOVE THEE, PLOT LEVEL	64
10.	SOPHISTICATED-NAIVE ENTROPY COMPARISONS LOVE THEE, SHOT LEVEL	64
11.	PHOEBE-LOVE THEE ENTROPY COMPARISONS SOPHISTICATED AUDIENCE, PLOT LEVEL	66
12.	PHOEBE-LOVE THEE ENTROPY COMPARISONS SOPHISTICATED AUDIENCE, SHOT LEVEL	66
13.	PHOEBE-LOVE THEE ENTROPY COMPARISONS NAIVE AUDIENCE, PLOT LEVEL	67
14.	PHOEBE-LOVE THEE ENTROPY COMPARISONS NAIVE AUDIENCE, SHOT LEVEL	67

CHAPTER I

INTRODUCTORY DISCUSSION

The primary purpose of the research reported in this thesis is the development of a new test instrument with which we can explore the interaction among different kinds of film (or audio-visual messages), different kinds of audiences, and expectations about what is going to happen next in films.

Experimental Research in Film

Of all art forms, the motion picture should be the delight of the "scientific" researcher and theory builder. Here is an art founded in science, a stimulus exactly repeatable, embodied in a form which can be examined by all types of gadgets; we can count the shots in the film, the frames in the shot, the movement within or between shots; we can count production costs or ticket sales. But when we are done, are we any closer to understanding the film experience? Past empirical research in film does not seem to indicate that we are.

If you exclude educational film research of the "which of these methods is best" type, and social-effects-oriented research of the "does filmed violence harm children" type, you are left with two general kinds of film research: laboratory analysis of simple forms[1] and case studies.[2] On the one hand, very simple film forms, generally

---

[1] E.g.: Joseph M. Foley, "The Bilateral Effect of Film Context," (unpublished M.A. thesis, University of Iowa, 1966); Roger Penn, "An Experimental Study of the Meaning of Cutting-Rate Variables in Motion Pictures" (unpublished Ph.D. dissertation, University of Iowa, 1967).

[2] E.g.: Edward S. Perry, "A Contextual Study of Michelangelo Antonioni's Film *L'eclisse*" (unpublished Ph.D. dissertation, University of Iowa, 1968).

only a few shots in length, are manipulated in a laboratory situation. Experimenters typically conclude that the film is more complex than their model supposed, and warn that their results probably cannot be generalized. On the other hand, careful study of complex, "real" film forms (films designed to be shown to a paying audience) has generally been limited to case history analyses of individual works. While these studies have sometimes been perceptive elucidatians of how a particular film may work to produce an effect, they offer no reason to suppose that the workings of that particular film are examples of a general pattern.

Although fruitful research can still be done along both of these lines, it seems to me that there is a need for a different kind of empirical research in film. We need to be able to analyze objectively the responses of large audiences of different types to "real" films. We need a generalized way of describing audience response in relation to films of very different types: theatrical, educational, animated, experimental, etc. We need a tool for testing the validity and generality of the insights of film theorists. We need to find some way to bridge the gap between the small steps of psychophysical research and the giant leaps of men like McLuhan.

I would like to discuss some insights suggested by information theory which seem to me to lead to a research strategy designed to meet some of these needs.

Information Theory and Audience Response

I think the concepts of information theory[3] can be used to generate more generally useful and relevant understandings of the type sought by laboratory experimenters, but based on a large number of "real" films and "real" situations of the type analyzed by the case historians.

Consider an observer watching a film. He is exposed to a linear sequence of sounds and images, which may range from essentially static to rapidly changing. He comes to the viewing experience with a set of expectations about what is going to happen. These expectations are based, among other things, on his past experience with film, his general knowledge of films (film literacy, if you will), and his expectations about this particular film. I assume that, unconsciously if not consciously, he attributes to the filmmaker a range of choices and makes predictions about their relative probability. That is, he expects that the filmmaker will do certain kinds of things in M*A*S*H that he would not be likely to do in Chitty-Chitty-Bang-Bang.

As he watches the film he gets information about what is happening and this affects his predictions about what is going to happen next (both immediately--in the next shot--and in the film as a whole). This interaction between audience expectations and actual

---

[3]See, for example, Allan R. Broadhurst and Donald K. Darnell, "An Introduction to Cybernetics and Information Theory," in Foundations of Communication Theory, ed. by Kenneth K. Sereno and C. David Mortensen (New York: Harper and Row, 1970), pp. 59-72.

outcomes in the film is, I believe, a major determinant of audience judgments of meaning and value in the film. (It may be necessary to consider a third interacting factor: audience <u>desires</u> as opposed to <u>expectations</u>. I have decided to ignore this factor at this stage of the research.) Complex interactions can be described using information theory concepts; now I just want to suggest, using simple examples, how information theory can provide insight. Let me postulate only two kinds of expectation in the viewer and three outcomes in the film relative to those expectations.

Let us say that the viewer can identify several things that <u>could</u> happen at a particular point in the film. Under one set of antecedent conditions (antecedent in the film and also in his general experience; there would be interaction here) he will say that the probability of outcome A is very high and, though he will admit B, C, and D as possibilities, he will say they are very improbable. Under a different set of antecedents he will say that the situation is ambiguous, he's not sure what will happen, and so A, B, C, and D are more or less equally probable.

Against these two expectations we can set three possible outcomes: A, Not-A, and X. (By X I mean an outcome not anticipated at all by the viewer.) Let us look at these six situations in the light of information theory.

(1) Let us begin with the situation where the expected probability of A is high, and A is in fact the outcome. Disregarding the concepts of boredom and banality (which would apply

cumulatively to choices in the film as a whole, but probably not to any particular choice), this outcome is rewarding. Although little information is provided in the information theory sense (where information means reduction in uncertainty), the viewer's world-view is reinforced--he "gets it right"--and that is gratifying.

(2) In the second (ambiguous) situation, knowledge of A reduces uncertainty and does provide information. Acquisition of information _per se_ is probably rewarding. More reward would be provided in this situation, I would guess, if the viewer could re-evaluate his perception of the antecedents in such a way that he understands why the choice of A was "right." The choice would then be "meaningful."

(I might add that it is in the filmmaker's interest to design situations that the audience will find rewarding, because a person will tend to repeat rewarding behavior; and if the behavior is watching "Laugh-In"--we're talking about the stuff ratings are made of.)

(3,4) Let's go back to the first situation and consider outcome Not-A. This comes as a surprise to the viewer and provides a lot of information; but it may be difficult for him to _use_ that information--to re-structure his meanings for the film so that the filmmaker's choice is understood. In the second (ambiguous) situation, outcome Not-A is treated the same way as outcome A.

(5,6) The last possible outcome, X was not anticipated

by either situation. Perhaps X comes as less of a surprise to the person in the ambiguous situation, anticipating A, B, C, or D equally--he is "hanging loose." Both viewers have to integrate an unexpected event into their meaning structure for the film. If they can change their perception so that they see that this choice, X, was available to the filmmaker, and further, if they can understand why he made the choice, then information, reward, and meaning should be high. But there is a chance that, for a variety of reasons, the integration will not take place; and this outcome, although high in information, will be low in meaning because it will be perceived as irrelevant, random, and frustrating.

Thus the viewer can be rewarded by having his expectations fulfilled, or by integrating an event that was unexpected or of low probability. The job of the filmmaker, I believe, is to elicit meaning from viewers. Now meanings, we know, are in people; meanings are not transmitted by the film. However, we can examine the information in the film and speculate about how it relates to meaning. Leonard Meyer relates meaning and information through expectation, uncertainty, and probability--the variables we have been discussing. New meanings arise, he says,[4] when our habitual responses are delayed or blocked.[5] His discussion is in terms

---

[4] Leonard B. Meyer, "Meaning in Music and Information Theory," *Journal of Aesthetics and Art Criticism*, XV (1957), 415-6.

[5] Cf. D. E. Berlyne, *Conflict, Arousal, and Curiosity* (New York: McGraw-Hill, 1960), p. 20; David K. Berlo, *The Process of Communication* (New York: Holt, Rinehart and Winston, 1960), pp. 78ff.

of music, but it is directly relevant to film. He says that the composer (filmmaker) can elicit meanings in three ways: by designing situations where the expected consequent is simply delayed, or where it is unexpected (novel), or where the antecedent conditions are ambiguous.

I find these ideas useful in thinking about films. Let me give one example. At the beginning of a film our uncertainty is relatively high, while the interior relationships--what Meyer calls the "intraopus norms"--[6] are being established. But uncertainty decreases and the probabilities become clearer (consequently information is reduced and, by extension, habitual responses predominate and meaningfullness is also reduced) as time goes on <u>unless</u> the filmmaker designs some uncertainty into the film.[7] This is probably one locus of creativity. Creative decisions (choices) are probably those that will be perceived as relatively unexpected but, once given, relatively understandable and therefore meaningful. (This might distinguish "good" novel responses from "bad" ones. I think this would be an exciting area for research.)

Clozentropy

If the statements I have made about meaning and reward are true, then uncertainty and expectation are important variables in film perception. But all of the statements I have made about audience

---

[6] Meyer, p. 419.

[7] Cf., Aristotle, <u>Poetics</u>, 1452a.

perception, uncertainty, expected outcomes, etc., must be taken as assumptions in need of operational definition and validation. How can we measure uncertainty and the range and relative probabilities of perceived choices in the film experience? How can we relate these to other variables in the film and in the audience?

We can have expectations on a number of different levels, roughly corresponding to levels of abstraction. On a very concrete level we can have expectations about how the filmmaker will frame his next shot; at the other extreme we can have expectations about gross theme or plot changes--for example: now the boy will lose the girl. And for each of these levels of expectation there can be varying amounts of uncertainty: from complete certainty that we know what will happen next to perception of the situation as totally ambiguous. If we had an instrument capable of analyzing the interaction of film and expectation, we would be able to address ourselves to a number of interesting questions. For example: For educational films, is there an optimal amount of uncertainty in relation to learning, and how does uncertainty interact with audience variables such as intelligence? Does "film appreciation" or "film literacy" mean that the audience has learned to attribute a greater range of choices to a filmmaker, with the consequence that any given choice may then be more meaningful? Or does it mean that film-literate people are able to predict more correctly than "illiterates"? And on what level of abstraction? If these ideas are useful, we might be able to evaluate empirically the many "visual education" programs or film appreciation courses being developed for high schools and colleges today. Are there any structural elements in film which transcend audience variables--that is, do some films produce the same patterns of uncertainty regardless of the sophistication of the audience? To what extent is the perceived information structure of a film part of the style of a filmmaker? Can varying critical responses to a film be explained by critics' different patterns of uncertainty, and by their differing ability to integrate novel events into a meaningful structure?

To analyze films in terms of these questions, the obvious choice for a measuring instrument is some version of the "clozentropy" procedure developed by Donald Darnell for the analysis of language patterns. Clozentropy related a standard measure of comprehension and language aptitude, cloze procedure,[8] with "an entropy measure derived from information theory which indexes compatability of an individual's responses with those of a selected criterion group."[9]

In the usual cloze test the subjects are asked to fill in blanks (every n^{th} word) in a verbal passage presented in printed form. They are given credit only for a word they get exactly right, that is, where their response matches the deleted word exactly.

---

[8] Wilson L. Taylor, "'Cloze' Readability Scores as Indices of Individual Differences in Comprehension and Attitude," Journal of Applied Psychology, XLI (1957), 19-26; and "Application of 'Cloze' and Entropy Measures to the Study of Contextual Constraint in Samples of Continuous Prose" (unpublished Ph.D. dissertation, University of Illinois, 1954), passim.

[9] Donald K. Darnell, "Clozentropy: A Procedure for Testing English Language Proficience of Foreign Students," Speech Monographs, XXXVII (1970), 36-46.

But obviously in some situations the response is tightly constrained by the context and the grammar as far as the text goes, and/or by the prior knowledge and social background of the subjects. To say the same thing another way: in some situations some groups of subjects perceive only a limited number of options for filling in the blank. But in the same situation other groups of subjects might perceive different options, or a broader range of options. And in other situations the perceived range might be very wide. So one can not only score a subject "right" in comparison with the author, one can also see how he adheres to the norms of any particular group of subjects; one can see whether a group *has* norms; and one can see how a particular text interacts with a particular group. But in order to do these things one must have a measure of stimulus or response uncertainty.

In order to calculate stimulus or response uncertainty we must "(1) draw up a list of stimuli or responses that might occur, (2) partition these into classes, and (3) assign a probability to each class."[10] Clozentropy procedure does this very neatly with language, treating words as the unit of response. No *a priori* judgments need to be made by the experimenter. Tests are easy to develop, administer, and score. Film, however, is different. One of the main problems of this research has been the development of a procedure for visual materials.

---

[10] Berlyne, p. 27.

I see three principal problem areas in the translation of the verbal clozentropy procedure into a visual one: (1) What are the units of analysis--the "blanks"? (2) Should the "blanks" actually be deleted, or should the projected film resume where it left off? (3) What form should the audience response take?

Units of Analysis

The most obvious unit of analysis is the _shot_. It is discrete, generally unambiguous and readily identified. In many films, however, sufficient changes take place _within shots_ so that certain shots cannot be considered elemental units.[11] But the shot is certainly an obvious place to begin. A cloze test for film could be developed by deleting every nth shot. The experimenter could use his judgment about making deletions within certain shots. One would avoid wasting time on philosophical arguments at the risk of introducing some experimenter bias.

Another alternative, since film is a time-art, would be to eliminate a certain period of time in the film (say 30 seconds) at regular intervals (say every five minutes). Experimenter bias might be reduced in this way.

A further alternative is to stop at obvious, subjectively selected choice-points in the film. (My solutions to these problems are presented below.)

---

[11] Cf. Andre Bazin, _What Is Cinema?_, ed. and trans. by Hugh Gray (Berkeley: University of California Press, 1967), p. 28 _et passim_.

Deletion of the Blanks

In the usual verbal cloze test, the blank remains deleted and the subject does not know whether his response was "right." This, I suspect, is an artifact of the usual testing procedure, using printed forms with each subject proceeding at his own rate. It would be awkward to provide the subjects with feedback about their responses. In film all the subjects are proceeding at a controlled rate, and it is easy to provide feedback. The decision between deletion or interruption is the experimenter's. If he decides _not_ to provide feedback, he must ask how much of the next shot (or whatever) should be deleted, and how _not_ knowing the filmmaker's choice will affect the subject's perception of his style, and the subject's response to later test items. If the experimenter decides to interrupt the film for a time and then continue where he left off--providing feedback-- he must ask how the subject's knowledge of his errors in prediction (perhaps continuous errors) will affect his attitude toward the film and, again, his responses to later test items.

Form of the Response

Perhaps the most difficult problem is how to ask the subject to respond, how to say "What goes in the blank?" With language, this is an easy task: the subjects supply a discrete word from their vocabulary. But there is nothing (at least nothing manageable) that corresponds to a visual vocabulary. Ideally, perhaps, we should ask the subjects to _film_ an appropriate response. This is obviously impractical. We might ask the subjects to sketch (storyboard) the missing information. This technique would present great problems with the analysis of the data, and with varying, irrelevant subject skills. We could ask subjects to select scenes from film supplied to them, or we could give them a kind of visual multiple-choice test with several alternative sketches or photographs provided for them. We could provide a common garden-variety verbal multiple-choice test. Or we could provide a verbal multiple-choice test, but one of a high level of generality, where the same foils would be provided for each item. (For example, one item might be: The next shot will be: the same image size (yes or no); looser ___; tighter ___; the same angle ___; from a higher angle ___; from a lower angle ___. The test would include many items focusing on action, editing, camera, dialog, effects, etc.)

Bearing in mind that one goal in the design of this measuring instrument is that it be capable of handling a lot of data from a lot of subjects about a lot of films, the most practical alternative is some form of multiple-choice paper-and-pencil test. But now we must be concerned with another variable: particular levels of abstraction. The experimenter must decide which one, or ones, he is interested in, from gross thematic concepts to very specific ways of framing and focusing the "next shot." There may well be interaction between various levels of abstraction, the subject's "film sophistication," and his ability to predict. But with a multiple-choice test, the experimenter artificially limits the

level of abstraction and range of choices available to the subjects.
A warning is in order.

Our ability to understand how a frog behaves by dissecting him is obscured by the fact that, through the process of dissection, we have killed him. When we cut up a film, and when we force an audience to make an overt response in place of something that is usually covert, if not unconscious--if, in fact, it exists at all-- then we are killing the film experience. I believe that this will lead to valuable knowledge and is therefore justified. But the artificiality of the situation should be borne in mind. (It is possible to ask whether an audience does in fact make either conscious or unconscious predictions while watching a film; and whether there might be some difference between predictions, expectations, and desires. I am in the process of designing research to examine these questions, but as far as this dissertation goes, they are assumptions.)

Design of This Research

The objective of this research is the development of a clozentropy measuring instrument for films.

In the balance of this dissertation I will address myself to the problems and possibilities outlined above. I will show how practical problems were solved through a series of pretests using a single film, and a final more elaborate test using two different films and a substantial number of subjects. I will show that the final instrument developed is capable of detecting differences in information and uncertainty patterns between different kinds of audiences viewing the same film, and similar audiences viewing different films. I will show that the instrument is capable of detecting differences in ability to predict correctly, and that these differences vary with the complexity of the film, the sophistication of the audience, and the level of abstraction of the prediction. Since this is not a terminal study aimed at deciding a question or supporting certain hypotheses, but is, if anything, an entering wedge, hammered by theory, into a whole new area of research, I will point out several areas of ambiguity and make suggestions for further research.

CHAPTER II

PRETESTS

The pretests were designed to try solutions to the various problems mentioned above, to develop a means for computer analysis of the data, and to provide the researcher with experience and data on which to base a more sophisticated analysis.

Design of the Stimulus

Ultimately, I wanted to study standard theatrical films of varying degrees of complexity (Love Story, Rules of the Game). To start with I selected the short film Phoebe.[1] I selected it because it was relatively short; it was in black-and-white (prints would be cheaper than color); it was well made in my opinion and used a variety of film techniques; it was relatively unfamiliar; and I thought it would interest a variety of types of audiences.

Phoebe is a narrative film about a day in the life of a teen-age girl. She is pregnant; she struggles with the problem of whether--and how--to tell her parents and her boy friend. The film is well done; it uses a great deal of symbolism, flashbacks, flash-forwards, and contemporary film techniques (but no fades or dissolves). It is a carefully made film with a distinct style. It is designed to stimulate class discussion (it is an "educational" film) of the problems of pre-marital pregnancy.

My first decision was that, however I decided to locate

---

[1] Phoebe. Sixteen-millimeter black-and-white motion picture, 26 minutes, produced by the National Film Board of Canada, 1964.

the "blanks," I would provide the audience with feedback about the accuracy of their predictions. I thought that it was more important that they see the filmmaker's choices rather than that they not be frustrated by knowing they made an inaccurate prediction. They probably could infer the accuracy of their predictions anyway, even if material were deleted. I decided that I would use the shot as the basic unit of analysis. This seemed a rational place to begin the research. The end of a shot represents an obvious choice-point for the filmmaker. In only two cases did I interrupt a shot. I also selected the places to interrupt the film subjectively. My experience with random samples of film shots, such as would result from deleting every nth shot, or at every n minutes, is that the resulting collection of shots can be very obscure. In this case I believed that the introduction of bias through subjective selection would be more than offset by selecting shots at meaningful places in the film. Future research should, of course, explore these other selection methods. (In the final test this totally subjective selection procedure was modified. This is discussed in Chapter III.)

Therefore, to select the places where I would interrupt the film, I viewed the film several times and picked places where the filmmaker, or the character Phoebe, had a choice, or where interruption would give me the opportunity to ask certain kinds of questions, such as ones about composition. The film, which is about 30 minutes long, was interrupted 29 times. (For a list of the exact points of interruption for this cutting of Phoebe, the second cutting of Phoebe as explained in Chapter III, and the cutting of the second film, How Do I Love Thee, see Appendix A.)

The film was interrupted by cutting to ten seconds of a black screen with the number of the response ("F 1," "F 2," etc.) on the screen in large block letters. This ten-second time proved too short, and was extended to fifteen seconds: ten seconds with the number and five seconds of black. Since I was making cuts in a standard composite release print with optical sound, the sound continued for 26 frames (about one second) after the picture went black. In some cases this was either distracting or "gave away" the answer; in those cases I cut the sound as well by opaquing the track with tape. In the very few cases where the filmmaker cut to the sound for the next scene ahead of the picture cut, I opaqued additional sound to avoid "giving away" the answer.

Design of the Response Instrument

The most difficult decisions involved the selection of a format for audience response. The questionnaire had two parts: the actual cloze procedure test taken in conjunction with the film, and preliminary matter designed to get general information about the subjects, primarily to rate them as "sophisticated" or "naive" film viewers. (Copies of all pretests are in Appendix B; of the final tests, in Appendix D.) The number of variables affecting the way different people respond to different films is legion. One of the variables that I assumed would have a large effect was "film literacy" or "film sophistication." I assumed that a "sophisticated" person would have some of the following characteristics: he would see a large number of films; he would value positively the activity of going to films; he would tend to like (or say he liked) complex, subtle, "arty," "in" films (a person who liked films like <u>Rules of the Game</u>, <u>Citizen Kane</u>, <u>Persona</u>, and $8\frac{1}{2}$ would be sophisticated, as opposed to one who liked films like <u>The Sound of Music</u>, <u>Airport</u>, <u>Dr. Zhivago</u>, or <u>Patton</u>). A sophisticated viewer would "get more out of" a film. He would probably be able to predict more correctly than a naive viewer. The first part of the response instrument was designed to enable me to explore for objective, quantifiable correlatives to "film sophistication."

Preliminary Materials

The preliminary materials at this stage of the research comprised questions about grade point average, number of films seen, favorite films, etc. There were also a number of questions based on Rokeach's Dogmatism Scale[2] (with the idea that there might be some relation between open-mindedness, ability to predict, and enjoyment of the experience). Data from this part of the questionnaire were examined both by eye and by machine. Since I knew many of the subjects for the pretests personally, I was able to determine that the number of films a person saw, and the kinds of films he liked, were a good rough index of sophistication. The machine analysis (a number of computer

---

[2] Milton Rokeach, <u>The Open and Closed Mind</u> (New York: Basic Books, 1960), chapter 4 <u>et passim</u>.

programs culminating in a series of rotated factor loadings), however, convinced me that objectifying the idea of "film sophistication" would be a long and complex task. The factors were not obvious; correlations were low or, in some cases, inexplicable. The small and peculiar sample made analysis and interpretation difficult. I determined that I would not pursue this area any further as far as this dissertation went. However, this part of the response instrument was extensively restructured for the final test, and I am in the process of analyzing the additional data further.

Color Patterns

Before I discuss the cloze response instrument, I want to mention an experiment tried but aborted after the first pretest. In spite of my interest in "real" films, I thought it might be wise to try an experiment with simple, abstract colors and patterns. This would reduce all the extraneous cues present in a photograph of a "real" scene. It would also provide an interesting parallel with research done with simple melodic patterns in music.[3] I designed short films with "vocabularies" of 4, 12, or 32 colors and patterns (red, blue, red with black circle, blue with black diamond, etc.), and with patterns (interrupted at every 10th color) that were either random, extremely simple (red, blue, red, blue, red, ____), or moderately complex (comparable to a kindergarten reader). The

---

[3] David Kraehenbuehl and Edgar Coons, "Information as a Measure of the Experience of Music," Journal of Aesthetics and Art Criticism, XVII (1959), 510-522.

patterns, which were obvious when jotted down on paper, were <u>extremely</u> difficult to detect when projected. The subjects became frustrated and angry. So this, too, was given up (for the moment at least) as a blind alley.

Cloze Response Instrument

In a preliminary test with a small group of film and broadcasting graduate students and another film (Peter Dart's <u>Peers</u>) I interrupted the film several times and asked the subjects to write out at length responses to the question: What will happen next? The range of responses was so great I did not know how to treat the data. Subjects' replies varied from the most particular to the most general, and from a few terse words to long paragraphs. I felt that, though these responses were interesting and perhaps should be followed up, they were, if not another blind alley, at least a side track. I determined to try something more objective and easily codified, at the risk of losing information.

I next tried to develop a completely visual multiple-choice test. The practice of writing a few visual items led me to believe that this was not the answer; or at least not a possibility for most cases. The problem was that the images (even my crude thumbnail sketches) were <u>too specific</u>. I felt that the subjects would be sidetracked by accidents of the sketch, and that I would get answers to the wrong questions. For example: at one point in the film we were viewing a flashback as Phoebe and Paul, her boy friend, enter an old house. I interrupted the film on an extreme long shot just as Paul comes up to the front door. At this point the filmmaker, instead of continuing the action, cuts back to a close-up of Phoebe in "real time." It seemed to me that the important alternatives here were not what the next shot looks like, but whether the filmmaker goes back to real time or continues the flashback; and whether he keeps the real time continuity or flashback continuity, or makes a "jump cut." (All these techniques are used in the film.) It seemed to me that the generality afforded by a _verbal_ multiple-choice test was necessary here; I did not want the viewer not to mark the foil that meant "return to real time" simply because he didn't like my sketch.

So I gradually evolved a response sheet that was primarily verbal (see Appendix B). For each "blank," I tried to give the viewer a choice of (1) a continuation of the action through a cut-in, or (2) cutting away to either something expected or something novel, and, in some cases, (3) a choice of staying with "real time," a flashback, or a flashforward. I gave the viewer three specific options for each "blank" and a common fourth option, "something else," to use if he felt that what was going to happen next was not included in my options. (I rejected the idea of a fifth option, "I don't know," as offering too easy an out for the subject.)

It appeared that the result was a useful instrument; however, first appearances were deceiving. The discussion below will point out several defects with this procedure and the remedies that I arrived at.

Subjects; Test Procedures

Pretests were run on three groups of subjects (with a few odd guinea pigs in between). The first group was composed of faculty members of the School of Journalism at the University of Kansas. (N=12.) The second was a group of students enrolled in the introductory broadcasting and film survey course at Kansas in the summer. They were about halfway through the course which emphasizes broadcasting rather than film. (N=11.) The third was a group of high school students from around the country attending a Journalism Summer Camp and Workshop. (N=24.) All groups provided verbal feedback which resulted in several changes in the procedure.

These groups were not designed as a sample of any population. They were chosen for convenience, and because I thought their diversity would provide me with helpful information about the testing and analysis procedures. Although I planned no formal tests of hypotheses at this stage, I expected to see differences between the high school students and the journalism and film faculty members on entropy for the various blanks and number of correct responses.

Subjects were instructed to complete the information sheets and look back and forth through the rest of the test. Ten to fifteen minutes were allowed for this; then the film was started. (Some subjects had to complete the open-mindedness scales after the film was over.) The practice film (portions of _Peers_) and _Phoebe_ took about forty minutes. The printed instructions (page 7 of the pretest) were reinforced verbally; "flashback," "flashforward," "close-up," and "long shot" were defined (the latter two illustrated with slides). Subjects were told that this was pilot research and that the experimenter was not interested in whether their predictions were "right." They had an opportunity to ask questions after the practice film.

Explanation of Clozentropy Data

A computer program was developed[4] which (1) computes the number of choices for each foil for each item (blank), (2) converts this frequency count into a percentage or relative frequency of choice for each foil for each item, (3) uses this relative frequency as an estimate of the probability, p, of that response to calculate the entropy, H, of each item (blank): $H = - p_i \log_2 p_i$, (4) calculates the entropy relative to the maximum possible entropy (which is a function of the number of foils) for each blank so that comparisons can be made among tests with different numbers of foils, then (5) calculates the information value of the foil, $I = \log_2 1/p$, (6) uses that to calculate the "abnormality" score, D, for each subject for each item, $D = H - I$, and finally (7) sums the D scores for each subject across each item to give a "subject abnormality" score. An example with data

---

[4]Again I want to thank Pete Klammer, Jim Frane, Bill Maxwell, and especially C. J. Bangert of the University of Kansas Computation Center. The program runs on the Honeywell 635 computer and is UKANCC: SFA58A.

from the pretest will illustrate the meaning of each of these scores.

Table 1
EXAMPLE: COUNTS OF RESPONSES

Foil	Item 4	18
1	6	15
2	37	11
3	1	11
4	3	10

In the pretest the subjects had four choices or foils each time the film stopped. (Again, refer to Appendix B for the questionnaire.) Table 1 simply counts the responses for each foil for items 4 and 18. For item 4 there was considerable agreement among the subjects that response 2 indicated what would happen next: 37 of 47 subjects picked it. On the other hand, item 18 was highly ambiguous: the subjects were almost equally divided among the four foils.

Table 2
EXAMPLE: PROBABILITIES

Foil	Item 4	18
1	.13	.32
2	.79	.23
3	.02	.23
4	.06	.21

Table 2 displays the result of the conversion of the counts in Table 1 into relative frequencies or percentages. It is used for comparisons among groups of varying size, and as the estimate of probabilities for the calculation of H.

Table 3
EXAMPLE: ENTROPY

Item	
4	18
1.02	1.98

The entropy table, Table 3, displays the results of the calculation of H. In this situation, with four choices, the maximum entropy would be 2.00, which would mean that the relative frequency (probability) for all foils was equal (.25). In other words, the situation would be ambiguous; if you were going to bet which response a subject would make, the odds would be even. Item 18 approaches this condition. Where there is considerable agreement among the subjects (item 4), the entropy decreases. A bet on response 2 in this case would be a safe bet.

Table 4
EXAMPLE: RELATIVE ENTROPY

Item	
4	18
.51	.99

For comparison purposes again, the absolute entropy is converted to relative entropy (relative to the maximum possible, $\log_2$ of the number of foils) and displayed in Table 4.

Table 5
EXAMPLE: INFORMATION/RESPONSE/BLANK

Foil	Item 4	18
1	2.97	1.65
2	0.35	2.10
3	5.55	2.10
4	3.97	2.23

Because betting on foil 2 for item 4 is safe, the knowledge that a subject actually chose that foil conveys little information, while the knowledge that he picked an unlikely foil, say 3 on item 4 (chosen by only 2% of the subjects) would convey a lot of information. These differences are displayed in Table 5. It is used to calculate the "abnormality"[5] of each subject's response on each item.

---

[5] Darnell, "Clozentropy," p. 45.

Table 6
EXAMPLE: ABNORMALITY

Subject	Item 4	Item 18
1	0.68	0.33
2	-2.95	0.33
.	.	.
.	.	.
.	.	.
11	0.68	0.33
.	.	.
.	.	.
.	.	.
47	-1.95	0.33

The Abnormality score (Table 6) tells you several things about the subject's response to that item. A score near zero indicates an average response; a positive value indicates that there tended to be agreement among all subjects on this item and that this particular subject went along with the group; a negative value indicates that there was agreement but this subject did not go along with the group. <u>Thus this single score indicates both the subject's agreement and the complexity or ambiguity of the item.</u>

Table 7
EXAMPLE: SUBJECT ABNORMALITY

Subject	D
1	4.7
2	-10.7
.	.
.	.
.	.
11	6.8
.	.
.	.
.	.
47	0.5

The final score (Table 7) is the sum of all the D's for each subject. Darnell's discussion of the sum D score is succinct:

> D scores from a number of response items can be meaningfully added, and the composite score obtained in this fashion for an individual automatically takes into account the relative difficulty of the item as it is reflected in the amount of agreement among the members of the criterion group. In short, the D score would seem to have many of the desirable properties of the normal z, although it is derived from nominal rather than interval data. If the sum of D for an individual across a number of response items is approximately zero, it can be interpreted that the individual's response patterns are approximately "normal." It could also mean that there are no norms for that kind of response in the criterion group. If the individual's score is positive, it would mean

that he conforms to the majority pattern in matters of
response choice. A large negative score would imply that
there are norms in the group to which the individual does
not conform--he is abnormal, incompatible, a non-conformist,
creative, or, at least, unusual.[6]

In the example given (Table Seven), subject 47 gave average responses; every time there was agreement on the choice of a foil, subject 11 went along with the crowd; and every time there was agreement, subject 2 disagreed: he picked a foil different from the ones the others picked.

Results and Discussion

Since most of the analyses performed on the data at this stage of the research were exploratory, I will present results and discussion of them together for the sake of clarity. As I reported above, factor analysis of the non-cloze data (with the purpose of arriving at objective, operational description of "sophisticated" and "naive" film viewers) resulted in a decision not to continue that analysis as part of this dissertation. The complete computer clozentropy program output for the three pretest groups combined (N=47) is reproduced as Appendix C. I will discuss below reliability, the entropy measures, the correctness of the subjects' choices, the subject abnormality score, and then a major problem with the response instrument.

---

[6] Ibid.

Reliability

The reliability of the test was assessed by Hoyt's method.[7] The reliability for all subjects (N=47) was .53. The reliability for the faculty group (N=12) was similar: .55; for the high school group (N=24), .44; and for the college group (N=11), .28. In my opinion (supported by my advisors at the Computation Center) the whole group reliability is satisfactory for a test of this type.

Entropy

Figure One plots relative entropy against the items or blanks in the film. (For the placement of the blanks in the film, refer to Appendix A.) Theory suggests, as indicated in Chapter One, that entropy would be high initially, then decrease as the audience comes to understand what is happening and what conventions the filmmaker is using. The filmmaker may try to keep this from happening by varying the message--using ambiguous situations, surprising outcomes, or delaying expected outcomes--in the hope that entropy perceived by the audience will also vary. One would expect to see some kind of saw-tooth pattern of variation.

What are the chances that this pattern is actually random? I think they are slight. By inspecting the film one sees a *prima facie* validity: high entropy blanks, (18,22) represent ambiguous choice-points in the film; low entropy blanks (4,14) represent

---

[7]Described in J. P. Guilford, Psychometric Methods (New York: McGraw-Hill, 1954), pp. 383-385.

Figure 1
RELATIVE ENTROPY, PHOEBE, FIRST CUT

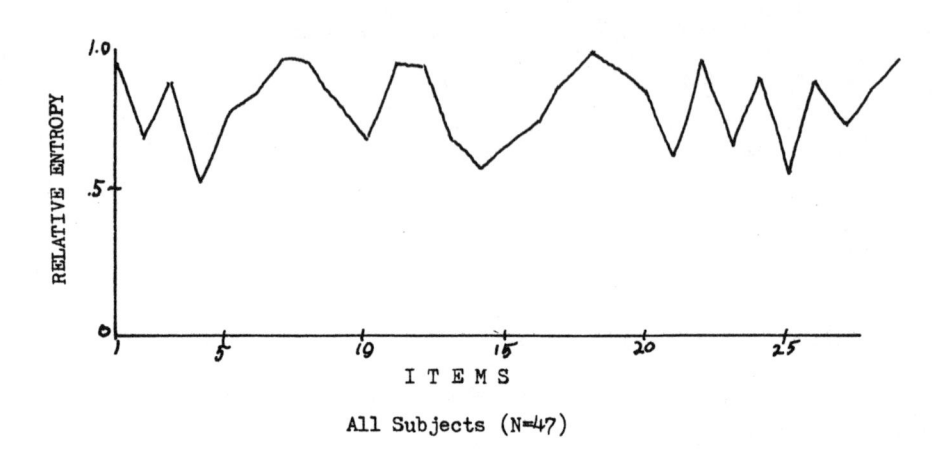

All Subjects (N=47)

Figure 2
SUB-GROUP COMPARISONS, ENTROPY, PHOEBE, FIRST CUT

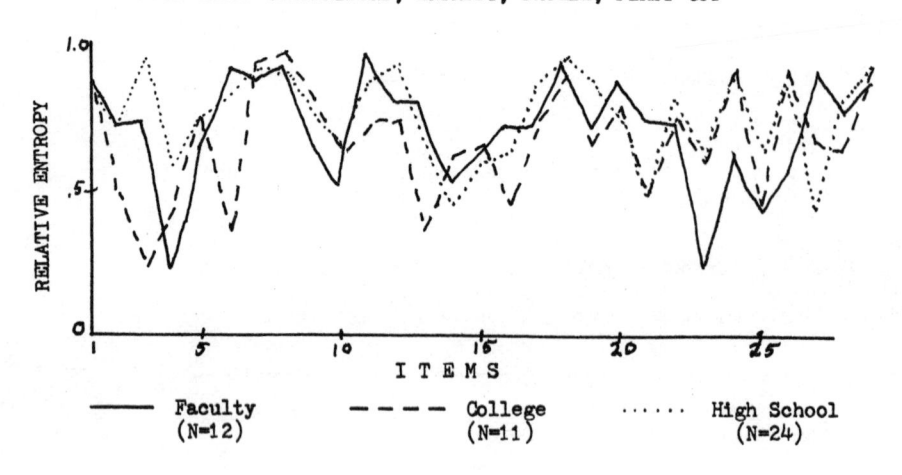

—— Faculty (N=12)   — — — College (N=11)   ······ High School (N=24)

obvious points in the film--the continuation of a scene, for example. And if one breaks the subjects into three groups (faculty, college students, high school students) one sees the same general pattern (Figure Two). This is evidence, I believe, to support the contention that the entropy measure is a valid indication of the perceived ambiguity of certain points in a film.

One validation for the testing procedure as a whole is the ability of the test to distinguish different entropy patterns for the same audience viewing different films, and for different audiences viewing the same film. At this stage of the research the numbers of subjects were so small and the groups so heterogeneous, that no further analyses were performed. Some differences, however, are probably "real" (at blanks 4 and 23, for example), and some reversals (where high school students perceive less ambiguity than faculty, as at blank 27) are suggestive. These analyses are continued on the data from the final test, in Chapter III.

Correctness of Responses

The responses can be scored either right or wrong according to what the filmmaker actually did "do next." (The correct response has been indicated by hand on the computer output "counts of responses" in Appendix C.) Theory and intuition suggest several things about this score: "sophisticated" viewers will get more items correct than "naive" viewers; all viewers will get more items correct later in the film than earlier (they will learn, in other words); "sophisticated" viewers will learn more than "naive"; in high entropy situations "sophisticated" viewers will get more responses correct than "naive." Examination of the results led me to believe, like other researchers before me, that things were more complex than they seem at first blush.

Again, because of the small number of subjects and the heterogeneous groups, these data were only looked at superficially, to suggest analyses for more complete data later on. The mean numbers of correct responses for the three subgroups are reported in Table 8.

Table 8
MEAN NUMBER OF CORRECT RESPONSES (29 POSSIBLE)

Faculty (N=12)	College (N=11)	High School (N=24)
8.4	10.2	10.5

The numbers are low (one-third or less of the number possible), the differences are slight, and, if anything, in the "wrong" direction (one would expect the faculty to do better than the students).[8]

---

[8]The following quotation seems appropriate:
"'Bunter,' said Lord Peter, as the kitchen door closed behind them, 'do you know why I am doubtful about the success of those rat experiments?'
"'Meaning Dr. Hartman's, my lord?'
"'Yes. Dr. Hartman has a theory. In any investigation, my dear Bunter, it is most damnable dangerous to have a theory.'
"'I have heard you say so, my lord.'
"'Confound you--you know it as well as I do! What is wrong with the doctor's theories, Bunter?'
"'You wish me to reply, my lord, that he only sees the facts which fit in with the theory.'
"'Thought-reader!' exclaimed Lord Peter bitterly."
Dorothy Sayers, "The Vindictive Story of the Footsteps That Ran," Lord Peter Views the Body (New York: Harcourt, Brace, n.d.), pp. 173-174.

Correlations run with number of correct responses against other information available were uniformly low, the highest (.34) with confidence that the subjects' predictions were correct. Other correlations were .28 with open-mindedness question 11, .24 with attention, .23 with classes in TV production, and -.23 with getting less confident as the film progressed.

Table 9
CORRECT RESPONSES, FIRST AND LAST THIRDS

	First 8	Last 8
Faculty (N=10)	23	25
College (N=11)	34	21
High School (N=24)	71	56

There is no indication that learning takes place during the film. Table 9 reports the number of correct responses for the three subgroups for the first third and the last third of the film. This could be the result of the complexity of the film, or of boredom and consequent inattention, or of the small number of items. Further research is indicated here, because it does seem reasonable to believe that, in some cases at least, you would learn to predict more accurately as the film progressed.

Let us now look at some of the relations between entropy and correctness. We find, in fact, several situations that parallel those discussed in theory in Chapter One. There are cases where everybody thinks the same thing is going to happen (low entropy) and in fact it does happen (2, 4, 10, 15, 16). There are other low entropy cases where agreement is high but the predicted outcome is wrong—the filmmaker does something else (14, 21, 25). And there are ambiguous cases (high entropy) where the (small) majority are either correct (11, 29) or incorrect (7, 18, 22).

I think it is safe to say that we now have a test which can detect, empirically, moments in a film which are perceived as either highly structured or highly ambiguous; and we can proceed to design and test hypotheses about the relations among ambiguity, expectation, reward, and meaningfulness. This task is not part of the present research, but some suggestions will be made in the concluding chapter.

Let us now look at some possible interactions between entropy, correctness, and "sophistication." One of the variables which might explain why people respond differently to films is their "film sophistication." I am, as I said, working on an objective, operational definition of the factors involved in "sophistication." For the purposes of this research I simply made gross, subjective distinctions. Most of the subjects in the pretest were known to me. On the basis of this knowledge and their responses on the preliminary matter of the questionnaire (especially the number of films they saw and the kinds of films they liked) I selected the seven "most sophisticated" and the seven "least sophisticated" or "naive."

Then, ignoring the continuity of the film and treating each blank as an independent test, I selected the five blanks with the highest entropy (assuming they represented "complex" moments in the film) and the five blanks with the lowest entropy (assuming they were "simple"). I compared the correctness of responses of the two groups of subjects on these items. The results are reported in Table 10.

Table 10
MEAN NUMBER OF CORRECT RESPONSES
SOPHISTICATED/NAIVE SUBJECTS
SIMPLE/COMPLEX ITEMS, PRETEST DATA

FILM ITEMS

Subjects	Simple (N=5)	Complex (N=5)
Sophisticated (N=7)	1.00	1.57
Naive (N=7)	1.57	0.86

The numbers of items and subjects are small, and the differences are slight and not significant. But this comparison is indicative of the kind of tests I wanted to make, and of differences that I believed existed in reality and that I thought my test instrument should be able to detect.

The Subject Abnormality Score

This score represents a comparison of a subject with a particular group, taking into account his responses and those of the group, the difficulty of the items, and his agreement or disagreement with the group. In teaching we are (unfortunately) always making comparisons and evaluating students against others or some abstract standard. It is possible that agreement or disagreement with a certain criterion group could be used to evaluate a student's progress in a film course, or that changes in the abnormality score over time might be used to indicate learning. One would have to proceed carefully, because the abnormality score does not distinguish between a creative and a stupid deviation from the norm. I have started some research to explore this area, but, like many things uncovered in the analysis of these data, I am treating it as irrelevant to this dissertation.

A few additional comments are in order, however. In some instances the score had a superficial validity. I knew some of the people who made deviant scores and they were the kind of people who probably would not perceive the film in the average way: practicing artists and filmmakers. Correlations were run between the subject abnormality score and a number of other variables. There was a slight relationship between abnormality and number of correct responses ($r = .30$). The only other correlations above .30 were with attention (.38) and frustration (.35). It will be necessary to interview individual deviant cases in depth, in relation to specific items, and to explore further the interaction of this score with other subject and film variables, before an understanding of its relevance will be achieved.

The Problem with "Gunsmoke"

At this stage in the research I had the opportunity to run Phoebe for a small group (N=7) of sophisticated film students at the University of Iowa. I was concerned because all the preceding data had been collected from one rather complex film. One of the goals of this research was comparisons between films; one of the major problems, the construction of foils for the response instrument. I decided to show this group another, simpler film in addition to Phoebe. I selected the final four-minute fight scene from the episode of the TV series "Gunsmoke" reproduced in the American Cinema Editors' film Interpretations and Values. The triumph of the good sheriff over the evil rustler in a western street-fight is a scene familiar to us all; and this particular episode is frequently used in film appreciation classes. I inserted seven blanks into the sequence, proceeding as I had with Phoebe.

The first problem arose when I wrote the foils for the blanks. I "knew" this was a simpler film than Phoebe, and I "knew" that the sophisticated subjects would get more items correct; I found it very difficult to keep these biases out of the blank selection and foil construction process. And I had no way of telling whether I was successful.

And then the subjects told me, unanimously, that they found it _much more difficult_ to predict _Gunsmoke_ than _Phoebe_. In fact, they did about the same: an average of 41 per cent correct, compared with their average of 48 per cent correct on _Phoebe_ (the other pretest groups got 33 per cent correct on _Phoebe_, on the average). But I considered this a serious criticism, and my instrument and procedures made it impossible for me to attribute the difficulty to the film, or the subjects, or my blank selection and foil construction techniques, or some combination of these. It was obvious that, before proceeding, I had to take another look at my "solutions" to the problems of constructing stimulus and response instruments.

CHAPTER III

THE CLOZENTROPY INSTRUMENT

Restatement of the Problem

It may be useful to restate the goals of this research as they were refined on the basis of the analysis of the data from the various pretests. The goals were:

(1) The development of a test instrument that could be applied to any film (or any narrative visual communication) and used with large numbers of varying kinds of subjects. The unique quality of the test instrument would be this: based on ideas from information theory, it would explore the ability of audiences to predict on several levels what will happen next in a film; it would identify moments of high or low ambiguity in a film; and, relative to a particular group, it would identify audience members who predict similarly or differently.

(2) The development of techniques for the analysis and comparison of large amounts of data.

(3) The data gathered would be useful in generating and testing hypotheses about interactions among prediction, information, entropy, meaningfulness, and various personality characteristics of audience members.

I will assume these goals have been reached if:

(1) My test instrument is easy to construct and highly general.

(2) Analysis of the data is feasible and comparisons are possible.

(3) These comparisons show:

    a. Differences in entropy patterns between different audiences viewing the same film.

    b. Differences in entropy patterns between the same audience viewing different films.

  c. Differences in ability to predict correctly; these differences varying with the sophistication of the audience, the complexity of the film, and the level of analysis.

(4) And if this research is heuristic.

  I also want to review at this point some of the variables that might affect the two dependent variables under observation, entropy of films and blanks, and correctness of response, and to comment on how I proposed to take them into account.

Variables Associated with the Stimulus

  Obviously one variable is the complexity or difficulty of the film as a whole. This was treated as an independent variable. Subjectively, I considered *Phoebe* to be a relatively complex film; I planned to select a similar, but simpler, film for comparison. (These subjective decisions were confirmed by discussion with several other film scholars.) This variable can be assessed by the entropy _pattern_ of the film and the _average_ entropy of all the blanks. It was expected that a complex film would have a higher entropy than a simple film.

  A second variable is the complexity of the individual blanks in the film (a simple film might have moments of high ambiguity, and vice versa). This was treated as an independent variable, assessed by the entropy of the blanks.

  A third variable is the placement of the blanks in the film. (This would obviously affect the second variable above.) The solution to this problem is a modified randomization process discussed in detail below.

Variables Associated with the Response Instrument

The two variables here are the level of response represented by the foils (specific-abstract) and the selection and difficulty of the foils. Problems with these variables were made apparent with the Gunsmoke excerpt. The solution, discussed in detail below, was to hold them constant.

Variables Associated with the Subjects

The number of possible variables here is very large. It seemed to me that the most important were these:

(1) Amount of exposure to films and television. With a large number of subjects this could be treated as an independent variable or groups could be matched with respect to it. I did not have enough subjects to do this. Exposure was one of the factors used to divide subjects into naive and sophisticated groups, but range of exposure for each group was great. The average number of hours of TV viewing for a two-week period for the sophisticated group was 15.17 (range 0-85) and for the naive group was 11.35 (range 0-56); the average number of films seen over a two-week period was 3.04 for the sophisticated group (range 0-8) and 1.33 for the naive group (range 0-4).

(2) Attention. A subject who was not paying attention could not be expected to predict accurately. I observed the subjects carefully during the test procedure and they all appeared to be paying close attention. Most subjects reported that the experience (for both films) was interesting. The assumption that any difference in attention between groups was random seemed, from these observations, to be a valid one.

(3) Prior knowledge. If the subjects had seen the film before, it was assumed that this would make a difference and those subjects were eliminated.

(4) Practice. Since this was a novel experience for all subjects I assumed practice might affect the responses. All subjects took a short practice test. The actual test films were shown several times and the order of presentation was varied to counterbalance the effect of practice.

(5) Verbal literacy. This might affect the way the subjects perceived the films or the way they took the test. However, almost all my subjects were college students or teachers, so I assumed a narrow range of abilities with negligible differences between groups. The average cumulative grade point average for the sophisticated group was B+/A- (range B to A); for the naive group B (range B- to A). (Since there might be some interesting interactions between verbal literacy and film sophistication, these should be explored in detail.)

(6) Film sophistication. As discussed above, this was an

attribute I wanted to treat as an independent variable. Since I lacked an objective method of indexing sophistication, I used all the information available to me about each subject (which was extensive as the questionnaire in Appendix C shows) to divide them into two groups: sophisticated and naive. The principal factors used in making the division were: number of films seen, kinds of films preferred, whether the subject had taken any film courses or made any films, and the kinds of reasons he gave for going to the movies. In only 7 cases out of 93 was the division doubtful. The classification of the doubtful cases and a sample of the others were checked by a colleague and film scholar, Professor Peter Dart, and we agreed in every case.

(7) Various personality variables. Some of the most relevant personality variables are probably open-mindedness and need for cognition. For this research, I assumed that there were no systematic differences in these and other personality variables between the naive and sophisticated groups.

The way these variables were treated for this research is not ideal. However, my goal was the development of a measuring technique. This goal could not be reached if, at the same time, all of the byways were explored. Something needed priority. I believe my results justify my decisions--<u>but only temporarily</u>. I have indicated other areas for research as I went along, and I have already begun exploration of some of these. In my concluding discussion I will make additional recommendations about new research priorities.

At this point I will discuss in detail changes that were made in the stimulus and response instruments.

Redesign of the Stimuli

Two changes were made: the addition of another complete film, and a different and more systematic way of selecting the blanks.

Phoebe is a narrative educational film designed for high school audiences. It is relatively complex, both in content and treatment. To test my instrument with a film which contrasted with Phoebe, I selected another narrative educational film designed for high school and college audiences: Cathedral Films' How Do I Love Thee[1] (hereinafter referred to as Love Thee). It was produced in color but I used a black-and-white print. It is a simple film. Its narrative is plain and straightforward, its message is blatant, and it uses simple, conventional film techniques, with many fades and dissolves (there are none in Phoebe). Its argument is against premarital sexual intercourse and it focuses on two sorority girls, one who "does" and one who "doesn't," and their two fraternity boy friends. Virtue triumphs, and the bad girl leaves town on "the midnight bus" while her boy friend marries the girl back home he "never even touched." (Students were delighted with this film as camp, and disagreed with the values it espoused.)

---

[1] How Do I Love Thee. Sixteen-millimeter color motion picture, 27 minutes, produced by Cathedral Films, (1962?).

For the pretest, I had selected the blanks by intuition, looking for obvious choice-points in the film. As I explained above, I found my biases entering into the process when I selected blanks for <u>Gunsmoke</u>. One obvious way out would be to select the blanks completely at random. I decided not to do this because complete random selection would be bound to result in both trivial and atypical choices. In a film of any length there are moments that are obviously important, that reveal something about the characters, the development of the plot, or the filmmaker's style. And there are other moments that are relatively trivial. I wanted to be sure, particularly at this stage of the research, that I included a large proportion of meaningful moments. So in cutting blanks into <u>Love Thee</u>, and re-cutting <u>Phoebe</u>, I used the following rules:

(1) Select a cut about 36 feet from the tail of the film, excluding titles—preferably at a choice-point.

(2) Count backwards in 36 foot (60 second) bites, selecting the closest cut.

(3) These rules should be "stretched" to include cuts representative of those in the film, including effects if used in the film, and including some obvious points of choice for the plot, characters, and/or filmmaker, when they fall near the selected point.

(4) Specifically regarding re-cutting <u>Phoebe</u>: if a cut selected in this way falls near one of the cuts made the first time, the original cut should be retained for comparison purposes.

The places selected for cuts in <u>Love Thee</u> and <u>Phoebe</u> are listed in Appendix A.

Redesign of the Response Instrument

The problems with the pretest response instrument were that it was difficult to construct, and impossible to control the difficulty or the levels of abstraction of the foils. I perceived two possibilities: construction of specific foils for each blank, as before, but according to very specific rules; or designing a set of "universal" foils that would be constant for every blank and every film.

A considerable amount of time was spent working on a set of foil construction rules, because I had observed that the pretest form, with specific choices and even thumbnail sketches (refer again to Appendix B) was enjoyed by both sophisticated and naive subjects. They treated it as a game. I was afraid constant, uniform foils would make the experience more boring. I tried many sets of rules like these:

Foil 1: Continuation of action by closer shot.

Foil 2: Continuation of action by cut-away.

Foil 3: Different action, previously introduced, same time.

Foil 4: Different action, new or previously introduced, flashback or flashforward.

Foil 5: "Something else."

Then for each blank in the film I would devise a specific choice according to these rules. But every set of rules I devised still left too much room for bias and confusion. So I reluctantly turned to the task of devising a uniform set of foils that would cover all possibilities and work for any film, and any blank.

The universal foils appeared to have one advantage over the

specific foils: they made it easier to have the subjects give more than one response at each blank in the film. They thus made possible two different kinds of analyses. There might be interaction between sophistication and kind of analysis in terms of ability to predict. For example, naive viewers might predict as well as sophisticated viewers at the plot or boy-gets-girl level, but they might not predict as well _how_ it was going to happen or what the specific shots would look like. I tried to develop one set of foils that asked for rather gross _plot_ predictions, and one that asked for more specific _shot_ predictions. This proved to be a surprisingly difficult task, especially since all of the foils should be independent.

The _shot_ level was the easiest. One obvious choice the filmmaker has is to build or relax tension through the selection of closer or looser shots. The set of foils finally decided on were that the image in the scene following the blank would be:

> _____ same size
> _____ tighter
> _____ looser

The _plot_ level was much more difficult. The final set of three foils was the result of many trials on assorted subjects with sets of foils varying from two to eight. Some of the variables considered were: that the next shot would show the action continuing, or an action in parallel time, or a jump-cut, or a flashback, or a flash-forward; that the action would continue with only a different view of the characters in the last shot, or a new character would be introduced into the scene, or the camera would re-establish a character already present but not in the last shot; or something completely novel would happen. The foils selected were:

   _____ this action continues
   _____ different action, same time
   _____ different action, different time

It seemed to me that this group, of all I considered, was manageable in length, with each foil of equal weight, and each foil independent of the shot foils.

So for each blank in both films, the subjects were asked to make two responses, one on each set of three foils:

 _____ this action continues   _____ same size
 _____ different action, same time   _____ tighter
 _____ different action, different time   _____ looser

See Appendix C for the complete questionnaire and instructions. This set of foils seemed to work well. The subjects seemed to understand how to use the foils, though there was some disagreement from a few sophisticated subjects on the application of the foils in one particular case. I am sure that would happen with any set of abstract foils.

Subjects; Test Procedures

Two groups of subjects were run at the University Film Association Conference in Madison in August, 1971. These were primarily college teachers of film, graduate students in film, and professional filmmakers. Four groups of subjects were run at the University of Kansas in September, 1971. These were primarily undergraduates in film, psychology, art, education, and various sciences. The Kansas subjects were solicited through personal contacts and advertising in the school paper. A total of 93 subjects completed the test instrument. Of these, 24 were judged sophisticated and 69 naive. After subjects who had seen one or both films before were discarded, there remained for Phoebe: 19 sophisticated and 58 naive; for Love Thee: 24 sophisticated and 65 naive. For some tests, for statistical reasons, the numbers were reduced to 19 sophisticated and 56 naive for both films.

The test took about 1½ hours. The subjects were allowed 10-15 minutes to complete the preliminary material (some had to finish it after the films); then the instructions were read to them and questions were answered; the practice film was shown; and any remaining questions were answered. They were told that this was pilot research and that they should not be concerned if they failed to predict correctly. Then Phoebe and Love Thee were shown, Phoebe first three times, and Love Thee first the other three. The sizes of the groups varied from 5 to 26. The projection conditions were barely adequate, but nobody expressed any difficulty in seeing or hearing the films, or completing the test.

Results and Discussion

The first goals (stated at the beginning of this chapter) were met: the test in its present form is easy to construct, can be applied to a wide variety of films, and the method of analysis generates useful comparisons. The final goal, that the research be heuristic, I believe has also been met; the ideas for further research generated by this study appear in the next chapter. The objective findings related to entropy and correctness of prediction are reported in this section.

Reliability

The reliabilities[2] for all subjects who had not seen each film before are reported in Table 11. For comparison, recall that the reliabiaity for 47 pretest subjects on the first cut of Phoebe was .53.

Table 11
FINAL TEST RELIABILITIES

	Plot	Shot
Phoebe (N=77)	.36	.41
Love Thee (N=89)	.63	.35

---

[2] J. P. Guilford, Psychometric Methods (New York: McGraw-Hill, 1954), pp. 383-385.

Entropy

The entropy measure reflects the amount of agreement among the subjects about the choices at a given moment in the film. The hypotheses were that there would be differences in entropy patterns between sophisticated and naive subjects and simple and complex films. The new foils also permitted testing these differences for two types of prediction, plot and shot. So that comparisons may be made more easily with other data, the _relative_ entropy figure is used in all calculations. A relative entropy of 0.00 would indicate complete agreement among all subjects about the choice of response; 1.00 would indicate an even split among the possible choices.

One way to assess the entropy differences is to look at the average entropy of all the responses. For example, it was assumed that the two films differed in complexity and that this would be reflected in greater disagreement about what was going to happen next in _Phoebe_ than in _Love Thee_. Therefore for each item the entropy scores for _Phoebe_ should be higher than those for _Love Thee_. The mean relative entropy (MRE) is an index of this difference. Table 12 presents the different MRE statistics.

Table 12
MEAN RELATIVE ENTROPY SCORES

	Soph.	Naive
Phoebe, Plot	.721	.833
Phoebe, Shot	.664	.783
Love Thee, Plot	.427	.552
Love Thee, Shot	.683	.752

We can see that the sophisticated audience always agreed more about what will happen next than the naive audience (lower MRE score); and that both audiences agreed more about shot predictions than plot predictions for Phoebe, but in the case of Love Thee there was more agreement about plot predictions. An analysis of variance was run with entropy scores for each blank as the criterion measure.[3] The dimensions of the analysis were films (Phoebe-Love Thee), groups (sophisticated-naive), and levels of prediction (plot-shot). The results are reported in Table 13. Critical F for the .05 level of significance (df 1, 50) is 4.03.

---

[3] The model used was similar to Lindquist's Type VI design, in E. F. Lindquist, Design and Analysis of Experiments in Psychology and Education (Boston: Houghton Mifflin, 1953), pp. 292ff., or Winer's Case I design (three factor experiment with repeated measures), in B. J. Winer, Statistical Principles in Experimental Design (New York: McGraw-Hill, 1962), pp. 321ff. The program run was BMD08V, a mixed model, repeated measures design with four variables: films, groups, levels, and items nested within film. See W. J. Dixon, ed., BMD Biomedical Computer Programs (Berkeley: University of California Press, 1970), pp. 586-600. A discussion of the general rules for these analyses may be found in C. A. Bennett and N. L. Franklin, Statistical Analyses in Chemistry and the Chemical Industry (New York: Wiley, 1954). It may be useful for the reader to review the derivation of the entropy scores discussed above in Chapter 2. The entropy score for a blank is based on the group of subjects responding to that particular item. The MRE score is an average based on the 26 separate entropy scores for the 26 blanks at each level of each film. The analysis reported in detail above takes films as the between variable. An argument can be made for taking groups as the between variable. An analysis was done at The University of Iowa with groups as a between variable, using a slightly different design. The F ratios obtained were smaller, but the same four were significant.

Table 13
SUMMARY TABLE, ANALYSIS OF VARIANCE,
MEAN RELATIVE ENTROPY SCORES

Source	df	SS	MS	F
Between	51	7.9365	0.1556	
films	1	1.1208	1.1208	8.223*
error	50	6.8157	0.1363	
Within	156	6.9267	0.0444	
groups	1	0.5843	0.5843	38.441*
groups/films	1	0.0044	0.0044	0.2894
error	50	0.7621	0.0152	
levels	1	0.3952	0.3952	41.6000*
films/levels	1	1.0325	1.0325	14.1244*
error	50	3.6549	0.0731	
groups/levels	1	0.0075	0.0075	0.7894
groups/films/levels	1	0.0125	0.0125	1.3157
error	50	0.4733	0.0095	
Total	207	14.8902	0.0719	

The difference between films was significant ($p < .01$); the differences between groups and levels, and the films-by-levels interaction, were also significant ($p < .001$).

The only significant interaction was between films and levels of prediction. Looking at the data in more detail (Table 14), we see that the MRE at the plot level of *Love Thee* was much lower than any of the other MRE scores.

Table 14
MRE SCORES, FILMS-BY-LEVELS COMPARISON

	Phoebe	Love Thee
Plot	.777	.489
Shot	.723	.718

This table combines both sophisticated and naive groups. The pattern is similar for each group separately. We note substantially more agreement about what would happen next at the plot level of Love Thee, with no corresponding difference between films at the shot level. There is little difference between plot and shot predictions for Phoebe, but a great deal of difference for Love Thee.

Subjects agreed more about shot than plot in Phoebe, a film with a strong visual style but which moved abruptly in action from present to past to imagined future. On the other hand, they agreed about the plot of Love Thee, which was straightforward and used conventional techniques such as a fade or dissolve to signal a change of time or location. The Love Thee shot predictions were more difficult to make--surprisingly, about as difficult as those for Phoebe.

Another and perhaps more meaningful way to analyze the differences in entropy at this stage of the research is by the use of graphs which plot entropy against items in the film. Figures 3 through 14 display various comparisons: first: plot-shot predictions, second: sophisticated-naive audiences, and third: simple-complex films.

In Figures 3 through 6 you can see that the sophisticated audience generally found both films slightly less ambiguous than the naive audience did; that for Phoebe the plot-shot comparisons are similar, while for Love Thee there is more agreement about plot than shot. The sawtooth pattern that was evident in the first cut of Phoebe (Figure 1, Chapter Two) is retained. Our discussion in

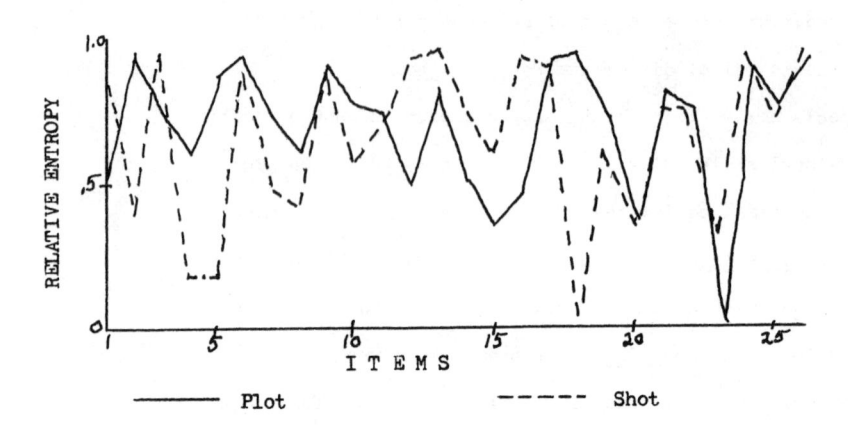

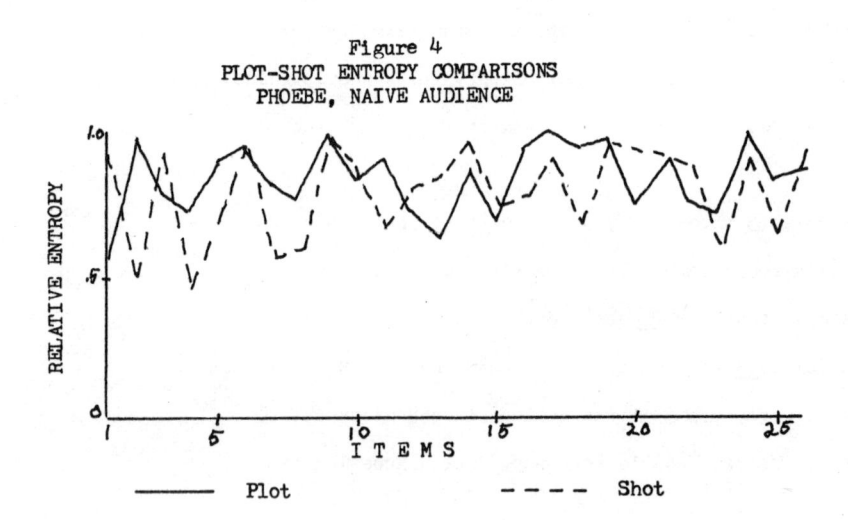

Figure 3
PLOT-SHOT ENTROPY COMPARISONS
PHOEBE, SOPHISTICATED AUDIENCE

——— Plot   - - - - - Shot

Figure 4
PLOT-SHOT ENTROPY COMPARISONS
PHOEBE, NAIVE AUDIENCE

——— Plot   - - - - - Shot

Figure 5
PLOT-SHOT ENTROPY COMPARISONS
LOVE THEE, SOPHISTICATED AUDIENCE

———— Plot   ---- Shot

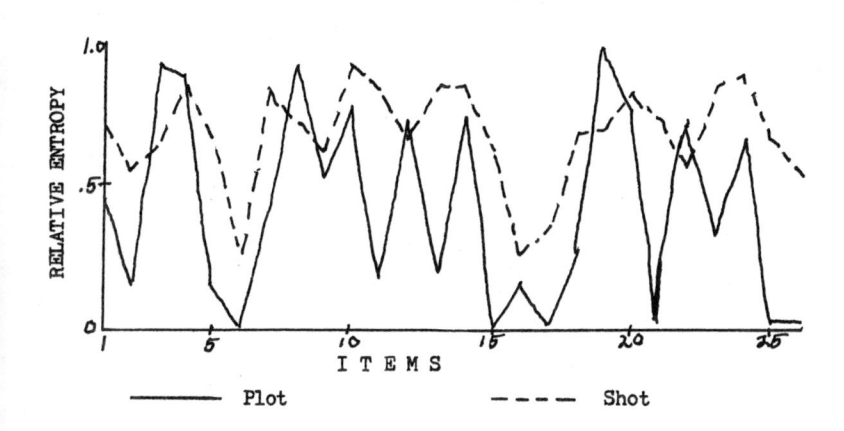

Figure 6
PLOT-SHOT ENTROPY COMPARISONS
LOVE THEE, NAIVE AUDIENCE

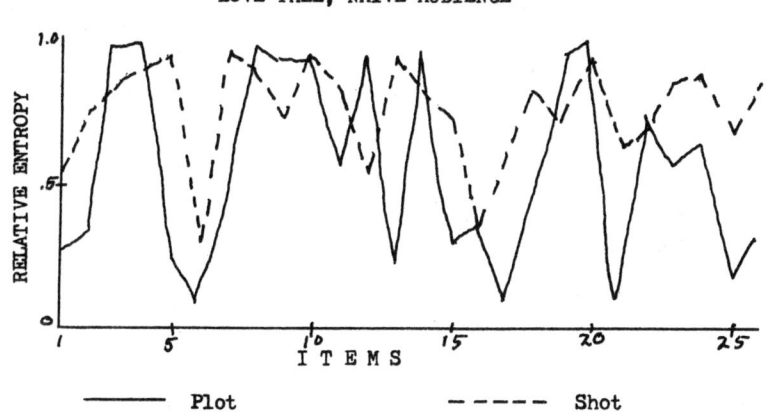

———— Plot   ---- Shot

Chapter One suggested that a work would become less ambiguous as the audience grew accustomed to the "intra-opus norms," and that the artist would purposely introduce ambiguity to maintain interest. This would result in a fluctuating entropy pattern. One would expect the more complex, "creative" film Phoebe to exhibit this fluctuation to a greater extent than Love Thee; it is interesting to observe that the reverse is true.

From these graphs you can also identify segments where both plot and shot entropy vary in a similar fashion (e.g., Figure 5, Items 4-7), and segments where the entropy diverges--where there is agreement at one level but not at another (e.g., Figure 5, Items 12-14).

These graphs support the results of the analysis of variance, that the difference in ambiguity between plot and shot predictions is observed primarily at the level of the simple film. Next, Figures 7 through 10 compare sophisticated and naive audiences on the two types of prediction for each film.

We see at once that the sophisticated audience almost always agreed more than the naive audience, and in some cases in the complex film there was substantially more agreement among the sophisticated audience members (Figure 7, Items 15, 20, and 23; Figure 8, Items 4, 5, 18, 20, and 23). For the simple film, although there is a difference between the mean entropy scores, the overall pattern is quite similar for both sophisticated and naive audiences. These graphs indicate that, although the analysis of variance did not show a significant interaction between groups and films, this might be an area worth exploring in the future.

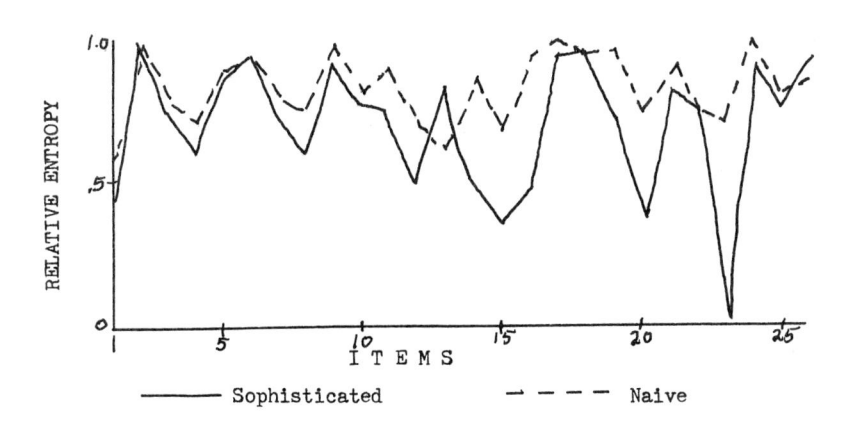

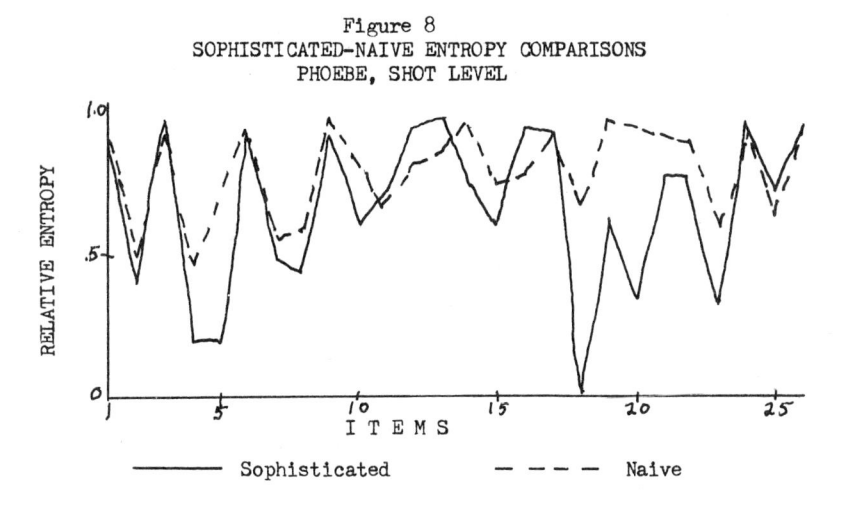

Figure 7
SOPHISTICATED-NAIVE ENTROPY COMPARISONS
PHOEBE, PLOT LEVEL

——— Sophisticated   — — — Naive

Figure 8
SOPHISTICATED-NAIVE ENTROPY COMPARISONS
PHOEBE, SHOT LEVEL

——— Sophisticated   — — — Naive

Figure 9
SOPHISTICATED-NAIVE ENTROPY COMPARISONS
LOVE THEE, PLOT LEVEL

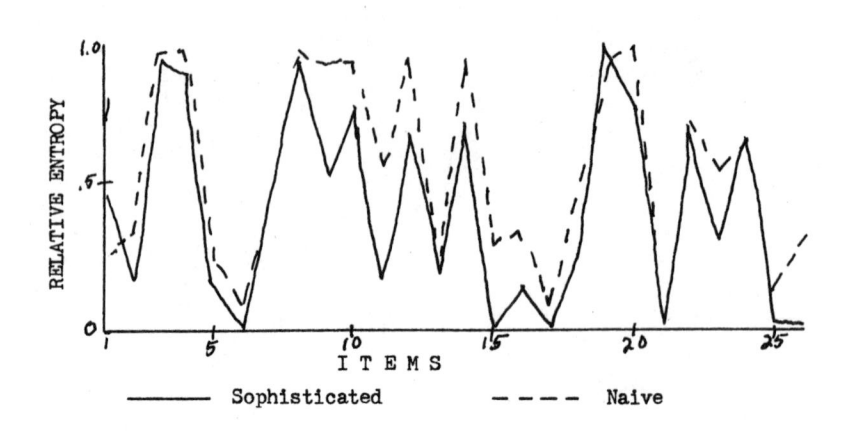

Figure 10
SOPHISTICATED-NAIVE ENTROPY COMPARISONS
LOVE THEE, SHOT LEVEL

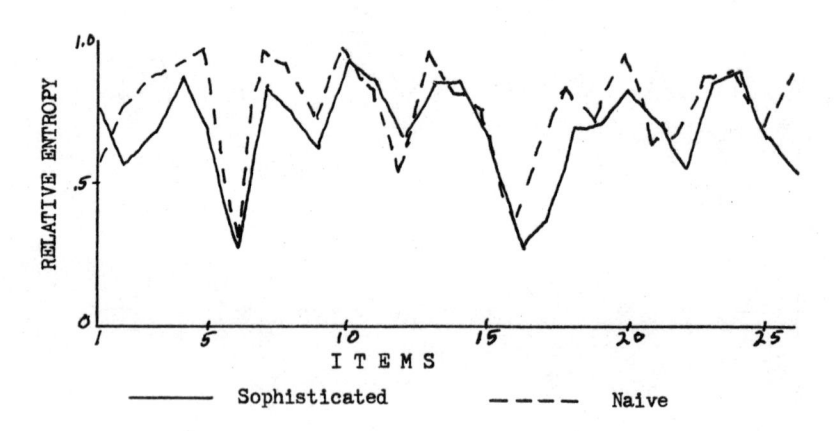

The final set of graphs, Figures 11 through 14, compares the complex film Phoebe with the simple film Love Thee.

It is obvious that for both audiences the plot of Phoebe is more ambiguous than that of Love Thee. It is also obvious that the differences between films in ambiguity of shot predictions are relatively slight. This conforms with the differences discussed above.

One of the goals of this research was to show different entropy patterns between different audiences viewing different films and responding at two levels of prediction. The results presented above indicate that this has been achieved, with the qualification that there is an interaction between film complexity and level of prediction.

The differences between sophisticated and naive audiences, though significant, are smaller and less consistent than one might expect. There are several possible explanations for this. One is that sophisticated and naive audiences do not differ a great deal in the way they predict. A second possible explanation and, I believe, a more likely one relates to the division of subjects into sophisticated and naive groups. As I reported in Chapter Two, it would appear that film sophistication is a complex, multi-dimensional variable, one that will be difficult to define operationally. I believe that there are different ways to classify level of sophistication that would have equal face validity but result in different entropy patterns. In the next chapter I will suggest some research designed to explore these possibilities.

66

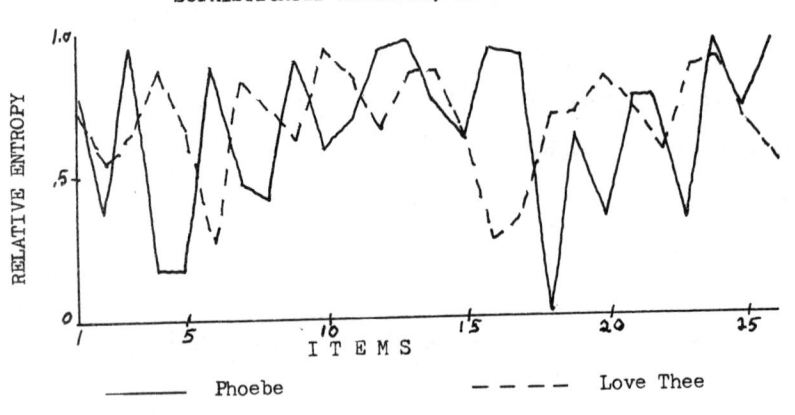

Figure 11
PHOEBE-LOVE THEE ENTROPY COMPARISONS
SOPHISTICATED AUDIENCE, PLOT LEVEL

——— Phoebe   – – – – Love Thee

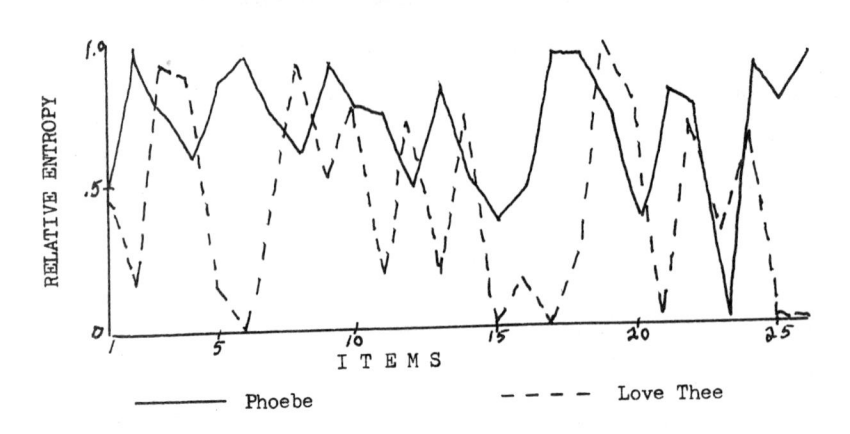

Figure 12
PHOEBE-LOVE THEE ENTROPY COMPARISONS
SOPHISTICATED AUDIENCE, SHOT LEVEL

——— Phoebe   – – – – Love Thee

Figure 13
PHOEBE-LOVE THEE ENTROPY COMPARISONS
NAIVE AUDIENCE, PLOT LEVEL

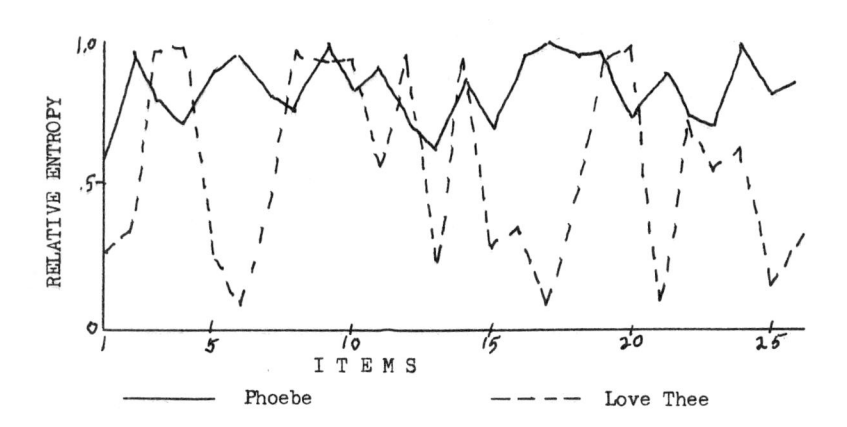

Figure 14
PHOEBE-LOVE THEE ENTROPY COMPARISONS
NAIVE AUDIENCE, SHOT LEVEL

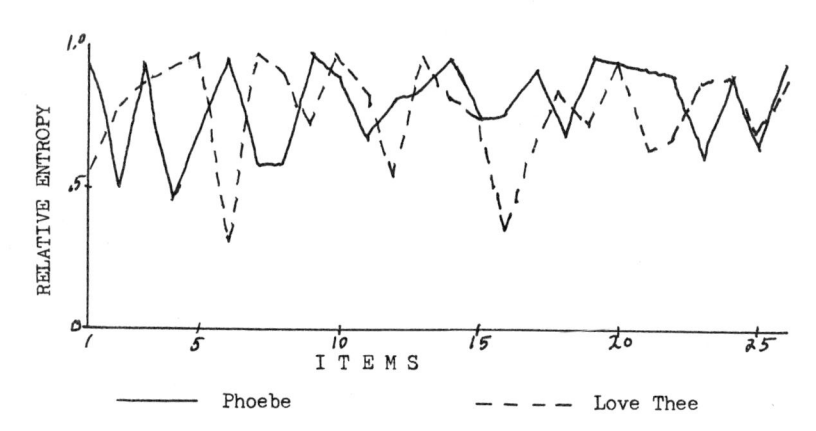

Correctness of Response

A goal of this dissertation which is closely related to the analyses described above was to show that there are differences in ability to predict _correctly_ and that these differences also vary with the complexity of the film, the variables being predicted, and the sophistication of the audience. Results relevant to this goal are reported and discussed in this section.

The mean number of correct responses and the variances for both sophisticated and naive subjects at the plot and shot levels of both films are presented in Table 15.

Table 15
MEAN NUMBER OF CORRECT
RESPONSES AND VARIANCES

	Soph.	Naive
Phoebe, Plot	13.32	11.27
	4.01	6.45
Phoebe, Shot	13.21	11.71
	4.27	7.95
Love Thee, Plot	19.00	17.70
	4.63	8.46
Love Thee, Shot	14.32	13.84
	8.85	6.17

The differences are in the direction one would expect: the sophisticated audience does consistently better than the naive; both audiences get more items correct on the simple film than the complex; both audiences get more plot than shot items correct. An analysis of variance similar to that run for the mean relative entropy measures was run with number of correct responses as the criterion measure.[4] The dimensions of the analysis were subjects (sophisticated-naive), films (Phoebe-Love Thee), and level of prediction (plot-shot). The results of this analysis are reported in Table 16. Critical F for the .05 level of significance (df 1, 73) is approximately 3.98.

Table 16
SUMMARY TABLE, ANALYSIS OF VARIANCE,
NUMBER OF CORRECT RESPONSES

Source	df	SS	MS	F
Between	74	1011.17	13.66	
subjects	1	100.54	100.54	8.06*
error	73	910.63	12.47	
Within	225	3002.50	13.34	
films	1	834.92	834.92	153.81*
subjects/films	1	11.04	11.04	2.03
error	73	396.25	5.42	
levels	1	238.49	238.49	49.93*
subjects/levels	1	6.74	6.74	1.41
error	73	348.68	4.78	
films/levels	1	279.83	279.83	53.25*
subjects/films/levels	1	0.27	0.27	0.05
error	73	383.62	5.26	
Total	299	4013.67	13.42	

Again, we see significant differences between subjects ($p < .01$), and films, levels, and films-by-levels interaction ($p < .001$).

---

[4] The model used was similar to Lindquist's Type VI design (Lindquist, pp. 292ff.) or Winer's Case I design (Winer, pp. 321ff., and unequal group size modification, pp. 374ff.). The program run was Clark University's ANOVAT, revised by Allan Press and Kris Arheart, Kansas State University.

Looking more closely at the data (Table 17), we observe
the same kind of interaction here that we did with the entropy scores
(Table 14).

Table 17
MEAN NUMBER OF CORRECT RESPONSES,
FILMS-BY-LEVELS COMPARISON

	Phoebe	Love Thee
Plot	12.29	18.35
Shot	12.46	14.08

This table combines both sophisticated and naive groups. The pattern
is again similar for each group separately. Both groups find it much
easier to predict correctly at the plot level of Love Thee than for
any of the other three categories. This parallels the results with the
mean relative entropy scores reported above. In contrast to those
results, however, here we see that the shot level of Love Thee was
also easier to predict correctly than the shot level of Phoebe
($p < .01$).

Looking at the differences between sophisticated and naive
viewers, we see that in every case the obtained mean for the sophisticated group is higher than that for the naive group (Table 15).
This is an expected finding; what is surprising is that the differences
are so small. The sophisticated viewers average less than two more
correct than the naive viewers; one would expect them to do better.
This is particularly true of the shot level predictions for Love Thee.
Here the naive viewers do almost as well as their sophisticated
counterparts. The structure, composition, and editing of Love Thee

is "by the book." It should have been easy for the sophisticated viewers to "call the shots" in this film. I can think of several explanations for the closeness of the results, none of which I find satisfactory.

The first explanation is that it might be more difficult for sophisticated viewers to predict shots when the film lacks a definite visual style. Perhaps the sophisticated viewers expected more visual variety or novelty from the filmmaker and their predictions were incorrect because they tried to improve on him.

The second explanation is that the sophisticated people might have been so amused by the banality of the images in <u>Love Thee</u> that they didn't take it seriously, and their responses reflect a lack of concentration.

Of course, a third possible explanation is that sophisticated people in fact are not able to predict with much greater accuracy than naive people. I am inclined to doubt this. My discussions with film students over the past years lead me to believe that some understand the "intra-opus norms" of films clearly and should be able to predict successfully. Therefore I believe that the closeness of these scores is another artifact of the way the subjects were divided into groups.

The closeness of the plot and shot predictions for <u>Phoebe</u> is surprising. I would offer as an explanation the fact, noted above, that the rapid shifts in the time of the action which probably made the plot predictions ambiguous also, necessarily, made many of them wrong.

Another point of interest was the large variance of some of the scores. Examination of the raw data revealed that in predicting the plot of Love Thee some of the "naive" subjects did just as well as the best "sophisticated" subjects; others did very poorly. This is additional evidence that the sophisticated-naive classification leaves something to be desired. These extreme cases should be analyzed.

I believe that the evidence reported in this chapter is sufficient to support the statement that ability to predict correctly varies with sophistication, film complexity, and level of prediction, and that there is an interaction, as with the entropy scores, between film complexity and level of prediction.

Three goals were stated at the beginning of this chapter. I believe these results justify the conclusion that the first two have been achieved. That this research also meets the final goal, that it be heuristic, will be demonstrated by the suggestions in the next chapter.

CHAPTER IV

SUMMARY AND CONCLUSIONS

Summary

A test instrument was developed for analyzing the ability of various kinds of viewers to predict what will happen next in various kinds of films. It was assumed that prediction--expectation--and its fulfilment or denial were related to the meaningfulness of the film. The test instrument was based on the standard verbal cloze procedure developed by Taylor and modified by Darnell. It was adapted to non-verbal material. It is not limited to the analysis of films, but can be used in its present state for any continuous visual narrative. The test is easy to construct and highly general.

A computer analysis technique was developed which generates a number of potentially useful statistics.

The test was validated by showing that it was able to detect differences in (1) entropy patterns and (2) number of correct responses between (a) sophisticated and naive subjects for (b) simple and complex films and (c) at two levels of prediction: plot and shot.

Conclusions

On the basis of the evidence presented in the preceding chapter, two general kinds of conclusions are possible. First, the clozentropy measuring instrument appears to be capable of making reliable and valid distinctions among audiences, films, and different kinds of predictions. It is a valid new technique for the empirical analysis of visual communication. The statistics generated by this procedure will make possible new ways of testing theories about film and communication.

Second, the data analyzed in the process of validating the test lead to certain conclusions. Because the data were not collected to test specific hypotheses but to aid in the development and validation of the test and the analysis techniques, these conclusions should be considered tentative. They are:

Entropy Patterns

Significant differences in entropy patterns were found between the two audiences, the two films, and the plot and shot levels of analysis. There was a significant interaction between level of analysis and film complexity. The highest entropy was generated by the naive audience at the plot level of the complex film.

Correctness of Responses

Ability to predict correctly also varied significantly with the sophistication of the audience, the complexity of the film, and the level of analysis. Again there was a significant interaction between level and complexity. The most correct predictions were made by the sophisticated viewers at the plot level of the simple film; the least, by the naive viewers at both plot and shot levels of the complex film.

Suggestions for Further Research

These suggestions will be divided into three groups: the first relates to a measure of film sophistication; the second to refinements and changes in the test instrument; and the last to uses for the test instrument in exploring the relationships between expectation and meaning in the film.

Film Sophistication

The results obtained in both the main test and pretests indicate that my division of the subjects into "sophisticated" and "naive" groups was simplistic and probably a source of error. Other ways of dividing the subjects (for example, by number of films seen, or by whether or not they had taken a film course, or made a film) might have led to different results. Film sophistication is probably a multidimensional construct with a continuous range of ability on each dimension. To my knowledge we have no empirical evidence of the number or nature of the factors involved. One might draw a parallel with the identification of the dimensions of connotative meaning by Charles Osgood and other researchers. There might be dimensions related to the verbal skills of literary analysis, and to the identification of the elements and structure of the film; dimensions related to the use of films (for example, as a social experience, an entertainment experience, or an artistic experience); dimensions related to the visual aesthetics of composition and editing; and so on.

Visual literacy programs and courses in film history and appreciation assume that a person with a low amount of sophistication can be moved to a higher level. To judge by grades, these courses are not uniformly successful. One reason for this may be our lack of knowledge of the variables involved. The identification and operational definition of possible variables cannot fail, I believe, to improve our understanding of the processes involved in visual communication, and consequently, our teaching of it. One variable is ability to predict; the clozentropy instrument will let us investigate this ability at several levels of analysis.

The Test Instrument

Familiarity with the instrument and the analysis techniques has resulted in a number of mechanical changes, primarily in the computer program.[1]

All aspects of this research should be replicated, preferably in the context of testing specific hypotheses or treating parts of the test instrument (such as the number and type of the foils) as independent variables. The lack of correlation between pretest and final test entropy scores on the 14 identical items must be explored. Does the pretest instrument, with its specific foils, represent simply another level of analysis like plot and shot, or is the low correlation an artifact of low reliability? Different films

---

[1] I will be happy to cooperate with anyone wishing to try the clozentropy procedure himself. Inquiries about the program, SFA58A, should be addressed to Supervisor, Applications Programming, Computation Center, University of Kansas, Lawrence, Kansas 66044.

and subjects should be used, and the subjects should be selected and the research designed to permit multidimensional analyses of variance to explore in detail the interactions suggested by this research. The independence of the plot and shot levels of analysis should be tested. Other levels of analysis should be used; for example, shot length or composition. It would be possible to devise a testing technique where the subject's responses would determine subsequent questions; for example, if the subject predicted that the next image size would be "tighter," he would be asked to choose among several close-up compositions. Films should be selected to permit comparisons of different treatments of the same kinds of material--a suspense sequence by Hitchcock compared to one by Truffaut, for example. This might be done by including in the test only selected portions of various films. This would be one way of getting information about more kinds of situations in a limited period of time.

On the other hand, long films and groups of films might be analyzed as wholes to explore ideas about style and the _auteur_ theory, on the assumption that a subject familiar with an _auteur's_ style would be able to predict more accurately than one who was not.

Certainly there should be research devoted to seeing what difference it makes _where_ the interruptions occur in the film. Several versions of a film could be prepared and shown to carefully controlled audiences. This might lead to ways of identifying "typical" or "representative" points in the film.

The correctness-of-response score can be used to assess

learning within a film by comparing the correctness of a subject's predictions early in the film with the correctness of those near the end. The same analysis could be made over a period of time in a film course. I am conducting some research along these lines now, with before-and-after tests in a film history course.

The clozentropy procedures generated three statistics which were not used in the analyses discussed in Chapter III: the information/response/blank score, the abnormality score, and the subject abnormality score (refer to the general discussion of the data analysis in Chapter II). The range and variance of the subject abnormality scores were greater on the main test than on the pre-tests. Superficial analysis of the data (more sophisticated analyses are in progress) indicates that some subjects are "conformists" with regard to, say, plot choices on the simple film, and "non-conformists" about shot choices on the complex film. These kinds of data may provide a key to some of the dimensions of film sophistication inasmuch as they indicate kinds of subject differences. For the non-conformists, it will be important to try to determine whether the responses are "ignorant" or "creative." It is one thing to predict incorrectly because you do not understand the structure of the film; it is quite another thing to be "wrong" because you perceive an alternate structure for the film, perhaps equally cohesive, perhaps "better" in some sense than the one the filmmaker chose.

Both the information/response/blank score and the abnormality score can relate correctness-of-response to entropy and conformity. (It will also be possible to tell whether a subject is biased in favor of a particular foil.) Use of these two statistics should increase the sensitivity and power of the test. It will be possible, for example, to weight a correct response in terms of the difficulty and ambiguity of the item. Perhaps there are differences in the ways subjects respond to an item of a certain difficulty or ambiguity when it is part of a simple film as opposed to being part of a complex film. Perhaps some kinds of subjects get most difficult items correct; perhaps other kinds of subjects get most ambiguous items correct. I believe that the empirical techniques of clozentropy analysis can be coupled with subjective critical techniques to discover the factors that cause a viewer to be sophisticated or naive, or that cause a film to be successful or not.

Expectation and Meaning

The discussion of information theory in Chapter I suggested some possible relationships among expectation, outcome, and meaning. The clozentropy instrument permits us to begin to explore these relationships; and that, I think, is of more theoretical interest and more potential importance than most of the research suggested above. For example, we can now identify points in a film where everyone agrees about what is going to happen next. Refer to Figure 9, for example. In some cases, as at Item 21, what everyone thought would happen, did happen. In other cases, as at Item 6, everyone was wrong: the outcome was unexpected. To what extent are different audience members able to integrate this unexpected outcome into their perception of the film as a whole? Does the meaningfulness of an item depend on the probability of its occurrence? Does the meaningfulness of a film depend on its entropy? Can we teach someone how to become a better predictor? Would this be the same as teaching him to perceive a greater variety of possible outcomes, or are the two antithetical? How can ambiguity and surprise be planned into a film? How can the entropy of a film be varied in relation to a certain audience?

To answer these questions will take judicious use of statistics generated by the clozentropy technique, coupled with valid operational definitions for meaning, meaningfulness, and value. The search for those elements in a visual message which contribute to its meaning and effectiveness will be difficult, but rewarding.

BIBLIOGRAPHY

Anderson, James A. "The Equivalence of Meaning among Similar Statements Presented in the Print, Aural, and Pictorial Media." Unpublished Ph.D. dissertation, University of Iowa, 1965.

Arnheim, Rudolph. [Introductory Notes to a Symposium on] "Information Theory" [and the Arts]. *Journal of Aesthetics and Art Criticism*, XVII (1959), 501-3.

Attneave, Fred. *Applications of Information Theory to Psychology: A Summary of Basic Concepts, Methods, and Results*. New York: Holt, 1959.

_____. "Some Informational Aspects of Visual Perception." *Psychological Review*, LXI (1954), 183-93.

_____. "Stochastic Composition Processes." *Journal of Aesthetics and Art Criticism*, XVII (1959), 503-10.

Berlyne, D. E. *Conflict, Arousal, and Curiosity*. New York: McGraw-Hill, 1960.

Breithaup, E. M., Jr. "A Study and Specification of Art Appreciation in Terms of the Structure of Visual Perception." Unpublished Ph.D. dissertation, Ohio State University, 1953.

Broadhurst, Allan R. and Darnell, Donald K. "An Introduction to Cybernetics and Information Theory." *Foundations of Communication Theory*. Ed. by Kenneth K. Sereno and C. David Mortensen. New York: Harper and Row, 1970.

Connolly, Richard L. "Predictability of Stereotyped Cowboy Films." Unpublished M.S. thesis, Boston University, 1956.

Cunningham, Robert P. "A Sociological Approach to Aesthetics: An Analysis of Attitudes toward the Motion Picture." Unpublished Ph.D. dissertation, University of Iowa, 1954.

Darnell, Donald K. "Clozentropy: A Procedure for Testing English Language Proficiency of Foreign Students." *Speech Monographs*, XXXVII (1970), 36-46.

Davitz, Joel R. with Beldoch, Michael et al. *The Communication of Emotional Meaning*. New York: McGraw-Hill, 1964.

Foley, Joseph M. "The Bilateral Effect of Film Context." Unpublished M.A. thesis, University of Iowa, 1966.

Gendlin, Eugene T. *Experiencing and the Creation of Meaning: A Philosophical and Psychological Approach to the Subjective*. New York: The Free Press, 1962.

Goldberg, Herman D. "The Role of 'Cutting' in the Perception of the Motion Picture." *Journal of Applied Psychology*, XXXV (1951), 70-71.

Gregory, John R. "Some Psychological Aspects of Motion Picture Montage." Unpublished Ph.D. dissertation, University of Illinois, 1961.

Haley, Jay Douglas. "Content Analysis of a Film: 'David and Bathsheba.'" Unpublished M.A. thesis, Stanford University, 1953.

Harrison, R. P. "Pictic Analysis: Toward a Vocabulary and Syntax for the Motion Picture Code, with Research on Facial Communication." Unpublished Ph.D. dissertation, Michigan State University, 1965.

Jones, Dorothy B. "Quantitative Analysis of Motion Picture Content." *Public Opinion Quarterly*, VI (1942), 411-428.

Kracauer, Siegfried. "The Challenge of Qualitative Content Analysis." *Public Opinion Quarterly*, XVI (1952-53), 631-642.

Kraehenbuehl, David and Coons, Edgar. "Information as a Measure of the Experience of Music." *Journal of Aesthetics and Art Criticism*, XVII (1959), 510-22.

Meyer, Leonard B. *Emotion and Meaning in Music*. Chicago: University of Chicago Press, 1956.

_____. "Meaning in Music and Information Theory." *Journal of Aesthetics and Art Criticism*, XV (1957), 412-24.

_____. *Music, The Arts, and Ideas*. Chicago: University of Chicago Press, 1967.

Miller, George A. "What Is Information Measurement?" *American Psychologist*, VIII (1953), 3-11.

Miller, William C., III. "An Experimental Study of the Relationship of Film Movement and Emotional Response, and Its Effect on Learning and Attitude Formation." Unpublished Ph.D. dissertation, University of Southern California, 1967.

Moles, Abraham. *Information Theory and Esthetic Perception*. Trans. by Joel E. Cohen. Urbana: University of Illinois Press, 1966.

Penn, Roger. "An Experimental Study of the Meaning of Cutting-Rate Variables in Motion Pictures." Unpublished Ph.D. dissertation, University of Iowa, 1967.

Pierce, J. R. *Symbols, Signals and Noise*. New York: Harper and Row, 1961.

Schwartz, Jack. "Semantic Analysis of Motion Pictures." Unpublished Ph.D. dissertation, University of Illinois, 1963.

Tucker, William T. "Experiments in Aesthetic Communications." Unpublished Ph.D. dissertation, University of Illinois, 1955.

Whitaker, Rodney. "The Content Analysis of a Film: A Survey of the Field, an Exhaustive Study of Quai des Brumes, and a Functional Description of the Elements of the Film Language." Unpublished Ph.D. dissertation, University of Illinois, 1966.

APPENDIX A

LIST OF INTERRUPTIONS

IN PHOEBE AND HOW DO I LOVE THEE

Interruptions in <u>Phoebe</u>. Print from Negative #5, Code #605602, 6/30/69. Footage counter zeroed at first visible frame of head title "Phoebe."

Feet	Frames	Pretest Blank Number	Final Test Blank Number
18	36	1	
35	30	2	
42	20		1
49	19	3	
81	29		2
86	22	4 (mid-shot)	
116	33	5	3
139	18	6	
167	29	7	4
190	7	8	5
232	19		6
240	28	9	
253	39	10	7
284	18	11	
296	14		8
318	25	12	
328	34		9
365	26		10
386	15	13	
404	10	14	11
437	2		12
451	11	15	
479	5		13
514	19	16	14
541	25	17	15
582	21	18	16
626	37	19	17
653	33		18
660	0	20	
689	27		19
698	32	21	
716	18	22	
731	36		20
774	18	23	21
787	29	24	
804	11		22
816	11	25	
837	2	26	23
876	21	27	24
907	10	28 (mid-shot)	25 (mid-shot)
941	19	29	26

Interruptions in How Do I Love Thee. No print identification.
Footage counter zeroed at first visible frame of title.

Feet	Frames	Final Test Blank Number	
47	36	1	
75	38	2	
118	39	3	
149	12	4	
183	31	5	
209	34	6	fade out--fade in
262	17	7	
291	33	8	
322	8	9	fade out--fade in
366	36	10	
405	11	11	
431	10	12	
479	31	13	
510	11	14	
547	12	15	
594	20	16	fade out--fade in
618	23	17	
654	31	18	
686	14	19	
724	4	20	dissolve
763	32	21	
779	33	22	
823	0	23	
862	35	24	fade out--fade in
901	13	25	
939	26	26	

APPENDIX B

PRETEST QUESTIONNAIRE

CONTEMPORARY

FILM

RESEARCH

217 Flint Hall
University of Kansas
Lawrence, Kansas 66044

Thank you for your help
with this research.

Please complete the information
sheets, then read the instructions.

INFORMATION

<u>Please note</u>: all your replies will be considered confidential. We are asking for identification only to be able to compare your answers now with your responses to films later. We will never identify you by name.

1. Date: _____ 1971   2. Your social security number
                            or student I.D. number: _____

3. Sex: male___ female___   4. Age last birthday: _____

5. Are you a high school student _____

          college undergraduate _____

          graduate student _____

          faculty member _____
             department . . . . . . _____

          other (explain) _____

6. If you are a student, what is your major, or career objective?

7. If you are a student, what was your Grade Point Average last semester?
   (D=1.0, C=2.0, B=3.0, A=4.0)

          1.5-2.0 _____

          2.0-2.5 _____

          2.5-3.0 _____

          3.0-3.5 _____

          3.5-4.0 _____

GO ON TO THE NEXT PAGE

8. In relation to your peers, how much time do you spend watching television:

    1. less time   _____

    2. about the same   _____

    3. more time   _____

9. Do you think the amount of television you watch is

    1. too much   _____

    2. about right   _____

    3. too little   _____

10. During an <u>average TWO-week period</u>, how many hours do you spend watching television: _____

11. How many classes have you had in television production? _____
    (Including classes you are taking now.)

12. How many classes have you had in television history or appreciation? _____
    (Including classes you are taking now.)

13. Name your three favorite TV programs (they do not have to be on this season):

GO ON TO THE NEXT PAGE

14. In relation to your peers, how many movies do you see?

    1. fewer _____

    2. about the same _____

    3. more _____

15. Do you think that the number of movies you see is

    1. too many _____

    2. about right _____

    3. too few _____

16. During an <u>average TWO-week period</u>, how many movies do you see? _____ (Including movies seen in class, but not including ones seen on TV.)

17. How many classes have you had in film production? _____ (Including classes you are taking now.)

18. How many classes have you had in film history or appreciation? _____ (Including classes you are taking now.)

19. How many films have you made? _____

20. Name your three favorite movies:

GO ON TO THE NEXT PAGE

Now, for a change of pace, we would like to know what you think and feel about a number of important social and personal questions. The best answer to each statement below is your <u>personal opinion</u>. We have tried to cover many different and opposing points of view; you may find yourself agreeing strongly with some of the statements, disagreeing just as strongly with others, and perhaps uncertain about others; whether you agree or disagree with any statement, you can be sure many people feel the same as you do.

Mark each statement according to how much you agree or disagree with it. Please mark every one.

1. It is only natural that a person would have a much better acquaintance with the ideas he believes in than with ideas he opposes:

_____	_____	_____	_____	_____	_____
disagree very much	disagree on the whole	disagree a little	agree a little	agree on the whole	agree very much

2. Fundamentally, the world we live in is a pretty lonesome place.

_____	_____	_____	_____	_____	_____
disagree very much	disagree on the whole	disagree a little	agree a little	agree on the whole	agree very much

3. It is only natural for a person to be rather fearful of the future.

_____	_____	_____	_____	_____	_____
disagree very much	disagree on the whole	disagree a little	agree a little	agree on the whole	agree very much

4. I'd like it if I could find someone who would tell me how to solve my personal problems.

_____	_____	_____	_____	_____	_____
disagree very much	disagree on the whole	disagree a little	agree a little	agree on the whole	agree very much

5. In a discussion I often find it necessary to repeat myself several times to make sure I am being understood.

_____	_____	_____	_____	_____	_____
disagree very much	disagree on the whole	disagree a little	agree a little	agree on the whole	agree very much

GO ON TO THE NEXT PAGE

6. In the history of mankind there have probably been just a handful of really great thinkers.

disagree	disagree	disagree	agree	agree	agree
very much	on the whole	a little	very much	on the whole	very much

7. In a heated discussion I generally become so absorbed in what I am going to say that I forget to listen to what the others are saying.

disagree	disagree	disagree	agree	agree	agree
very much	on the whole	a little	a little	on the whole	very much

8. If given the chance, I would do something of great benefit to the world.

disagree	disagree	disagree	agree	agree	agree
very much	on the whole	a little	a little	on the whole	very much

9. There are a number of people I have come to hate because of the things they stand for.

disagree	disagree	disagree	agree	agree	agree
very much	on the whole	a little	a little	on the whole	very much

10. It is only when a person devotes himself to an ideal or cause that life becomes meaningful.

disagree	disagree	disagree	agree	agree	agree
very much	on the whole	a little	a little	on the whole	very much

11. There are two kinds of people in this world: those who are for the truth and those who are against it.

disagree	disagree	disagree	agree	agree	agree
very much	on the whole	a little	a little	on the whole	very much

12. In this complicated world of ours the only way we can know what's going on is to rely on leaders or experts who can be trusted.

disagree	disagree	disagree	agree	agree	agree
very much	on the whole	a little	a little	on the whole	very much

GO ON TO THE NEXT PAGE

13. My blood boils whenever a person stubbornly refuses to admit he's wrong.

disagree	disagree	disagree	agree	agree	agree
very much	on the whole	a little	a little	on the whole	very much

14. It is often necessary to reserve judgment about what's going on until one has had a chance to hear the opinions of those one respects.

disagree	disagree	disagree	agree	agree	agree
very much	on the whole	a little	a little	on the whole	very much

15. Unfortunately, a good many people with whom I have discussed important social and moral problems don't really understand what's going on.

disagree	disagree	disagree	agree	agree	agree
very much	on the whole	a little	a little	on the whole	very much

GO ON TO THE NEXT PAGE

INSTRUCTIONS

You are going to see a thirty-minute film. We are interested in your <u>predictions</u> about <u>what will happen next</u>. At several points in the film, the picture will black out for 15 seconds. Please check on the answer sheet, opposite the number corresponding to the number appearing on the screen, the response that is closest to WHAT YOU THINK YOU WILL SEE NEXT. (What you think you will <u>actually see</u> on the screen, not what you wish would happen or what you would do if you were making the film.)

If you feel that what will happen next is not included in the choices you are given, mark #4, "something else."

Respond to each question. If you don't know--guess.

Give only one answer to each question.

Before the main film you will see a short practice film. Then you will have an opportunity to ask questions.

Now, please glance through the answer sheets.

LOOK THROUGH THE ANSWER SHEETS

BE READY TO BEGIN

P-1 _____ 1. girl in another room in the house
     _____ 2. girl outside
     _____ 3. close-up something on dresser
     _____ 4. something else

P-2 _____ 1. close-up girl
     _____ 2. close-up old man
     _____ 3. long shot girl and old man
     _____ 4. something else

P-3 _____ 1. photographer
     _____ 2. long shot girl and new person
     _____ 3. old man
     _____ 4. something else

If you have questions, please ask them now.

BE READY TO BEGIN

F-1   _____ 1. A picture on the wall
      _____ 2. close-up of the girl (Phoebe)
      _____ 3. long shot of the girl (Phoebe) in the room
      _____ 4. something else

F-2   _____ 1. close-up of mother
      _____ 2. medium shot of Phoebe in bed
      _____ 3. long shot of Phoebe in the room
      _____ 4. something else

F-3   _____ 1. close-up of Phoebe
      _____ 2. long shot of the mother
      _____ 3. shot of person on other end of the phone
      _____ 4. something else

F-4   _____ 1. long shot Phoebe through door
      _____ 2. this shot continues
      _____ 3. Phoebe's mother
      _____ 4. something else

F-5   _____ 1. back to Phoebe in the bathroom
      _____ 2. mother
      _____ 3. this shot continues, Phoebe walks away
      _____ 4. something else

GO ON TO THE NEXT PAGE

F-6
1. a baby
2. Phoebe in black dress again
3. Phoebe and her boy friend
4. something else

F-7
1. close shot Phoebe and Paul at door
2. inside the old house
3. mother
4. something else

F-8
1. high angle shot of road
2. close-up of Paul
3. close-up of Phoebe
4. something else

F-9
1. Phoebe's reflection in bath mirror
2. mother
3. Paul inside the house
4. something else

F-10

1. Phoebe   2. Phoebe   3. Paul
4. something else

TURN THE PAGE

F-11

_____ 1. Paul   _____ 2. Phoebe   _____ 3. Phoebe

_____ 4. something else

F-12   _____ 1. close-up Phoebe back in old room

_____ 2. long-shot Phoebe back in old room

_____ 3. close shot Phoebe and Paul kissing

_____ 4. something else

F-13   _____ 1. Paul swimming

_____ 2. mother

_____ 3. Phoebe and Paul in a flashback

_____ 4. something else

F-14   _____ 1. Paul

_____ 2. flashback to Phoebe and Paul in house

_____ 3. flash-forward to something Phoebe imagines

_____ 4. something else

F-15   _____ 1. close-up Phoebe

_____ 2. mother

_____ 3. shot continues

_____ 4. something else

TURN THE PAGE

F-16   _____ 1. long shot, kissing continues

_____ 2. Phoebe and Paul on beach

_____ 3. the three dancing figures

_____ 4. something else

F-17   _____ 1. the three dancing figures

_____ 2. Paul

_____ 3. Phoebe's parents

_____ 4. something else

F-18   _____ 1. Phoebe's parents

_____ 2. the woman in school

_____ 3. the same shot continues

_____ 4. something else

F-19   _____ 1. close-up Phoebe

_____ 2. flashback to Phoebe and Paul

_____ 3. flash-forward to something Phoebe imagines

_____ 4. something else

F-20

_____ 1. Phoebe   _____ 2. Phoebe   _____ 3. Phoebe

_____ 4. something else

TURN THE PAGE

F-21 _____ 1. the same shot continues
      _____ 2. close-up Paul
      _____ 3. Phoebe and Paul on beach
      _____ 4. something else

F-22 _____ 1. close-up Paul
      _____ 2. mother
      _____ 3. father
      _____ 4. something else

F-23 _____ 1. the three dancing figures
      _____ 2. close-up of Phoebe from Paul's point of view
      _____ 3. flash-forward to something Phoebe imagines
      _____ 4. something else

F-24 _____ 1. group entering a car
      _____ 2. Phoebe and Paul from the point of view of the three
      _____ 3. all in the car, driving
      _____ 4. something else

F-25 _____ 1. long shot car moving
      _____ 2. close-up Phoebe in car
      _____ 3. Phoebe and her mother
      _____ 4. something else

TURN THE PAGE

F-26 _____ 1. close-up Phoebe in car
_____ 2. close-up Phoebe in house
_____ 3. more bridges going by
_____ 4. something else

F-27 _____ 1. inside house, Phoebe enters
_____ 2. this shot continues
_____ 3. mother
_____ 4. something else

F-28 _____ 1. close-up Phoebe
_____ 2. close-up mother
_____ 3. this shot continues
_____ 4. something else

F-29 _____ 1. Phoebe goes to phone
_____ 2. Phoebe goes to mother
_____ 3. the film ends
_____ 4. something else

GO ON TO THE NEXT PAGE

Have you ever seen this film, <u>Phoebe</u>, before? yes _____   no _____

Now, please, some feedback for us. Please check as many of the words or phrases below that describe your feelings about this experience:

_____ 1. interesting

_____ 2. frustrating

_____ 3. stimulating

_____ 4. dull

_____ 5. boring

_____ 6. exciting

_____ 7. I was generally attentive

_____ 8. I was generally distracted

_____ 9. I was confident that my predictions were correct

_____ 10. I had little confidence in my predictions

_____ 11. As the film went on, I got more confident

_____ 12. As the film went on, I got less confident

Please use the rest of this page to write any comments you may have about this experience. Again, thank you very much.

If you would like to participate in additional research of this type, please give us your name and address:

APPENDIX C

MAIN TEST QUESTIONNAIRE

CONTEMPORARY

FILM

RESEARCH

217 Flint Hall
University of Kansas
Lawrence, Kansas 66044

INFORMATION

Thank you for your help with this research.

Please complete the information sheets, then read the instructions.

<u>Please note:</u> all your replies will be considered confidential. We are asking for identification only to be able to compare your answers now with your responses to films later.

1. Date _____ I.D. _____
(name, social security number, student I.D., etc.)

3. Sex: ____ 1. male   ____ 2. female

4. Age last birthday: ____

5. Status: ____ 1. high school student

           ____ 2. college undergraduate

           ____ 3. M.A. candidate

           ____ 4. Ph.D. candidate

           ____ 5. faculty member, high school

           ____ 6. faculty member, college

           ____ 7. professional film maker

           ____ 8. allied profession

           ____ 9. other; explain:

6. What is your major, career objective, or area of professional interest?

7. What was your grade average last semester? If you are no longer in school, what was your average the last semester you were?

     ____ 1. F   ____ 4. C   ____ 7. B-A

     ____ 2. D   ____ 5. C-B   ____ 8. A

     ____ 3. D-C   ____ 6. B

GO ON TO THE NEXT PAGE

8. In relation to your peers, how much time do you spend watching television?

        1. less time   _____

        2. about the same   _____

        3. more time   _____

9. Do you think the amount of time you watch television is

        1. too much   _____

        2. about right   _____

        3. too little   _____

10. During an **average TWO-week period**, how many hours do you spend watching television? _____

11. In relation to your peers, how many movies do you see?

        1. fewer   _____

        2. about the same   _____

        3. more   _____

12. Do you think that the number of movies you see is

        1. too many   _____

        2. about right   _____

        3. too few   _____

13. During an average TWO-week period, how many movies do you see? _____

14. How many courses have you had in film or TV history, appreciation, theory, or criticism? (Including courses you are taking now.)

        1. none   _____

        2. one   _____

        3. two   _____

        4. three   _____

        5. four or more   _____

GO ON TO THE NEXT PAGE

15. What was your average grade in these classes?

    ____ 1. F   ____ 4. C   ____ 7. B-A

    ____ 2. D   ____ 5. C-B   ____ 8. A

    ____ 3. D-C   ____ 6. B

16. How many films (other than "home movies") have you made?

    ____ 1. none

    ____ 2. one

    ____ 3. two-four

    ____ 4. five or more

On the questions below, check the one blank that best applies to you:

17. ____ 1. I go to the movies to "escape."

    ____ 2. I go to the movies for entertainment.

18. ____ 1. The main thing I look for in a movie is a good story.

    ____ 2. The main thing I look for is a socially relevant theme.

19. ____ 1. The main thing I look for is a star I like.

    ____ 2. The main thing I look for is a new face.

20. ____ 1. I go to the movies for entertainment.

    ____ 2. I go to the movies for the kind of thing I can't get on TV.

21. ____ 1. I like to see a lot of action

    ____ 2. I like to see a director's style.

22. ____ 1. I go to the movies for entertainment.

    ____ 2. I go to the movies to see something that stimulates my thinking.

23. ____ 1. I like to see a good story.

    ____ 2. I like to see interesting character relationships.

GO ON TO THE NEXT PAGE

24. ____ 1. I go to the movies to "escape."

    ____ 2. I go to the movies for the kind of thing I can't get on TV.

25. ____ 1. I like to see something familiar.

    ____ 2. I like to see something new.

26. ____ 1. I like a lot of action.

    ____ 2. I like a lot of thought.

27. ____ 1. I go to the movies to "escape."

    ____ 2. I go to the movies to see something that stimulates my thinking.

28. ____ 1. I like to see good acting.

    ____ 2. I like to see interesting character relationships.

29. ____ 1. I like to see something simple.

    ____ 2. I like to see something complex.

30. ____ 1. I have a favorite actor and try to see all his films.

    ____ 2. I have a favorite director and try to see all his films.

31. ____ 1. I go to the movies for the kind of thing I can't get on TV.

    ____ 2. I go to the movies to see something that stimulates my thinking.

32. ____ 1. I like to see good acting.

    ____ 2. I like to watch a director's style.

33. (Answer only if you feel qualified.) Name the three films you think are the "best" (for example, three films you think should be part of every student's education, in the same way he is asked to read Hamlet):

(Answer all the other questions.)
34. Name your three personal favorite films:

GO ON TO THE NEXT PAGE

35. Name your three personal favorite TV programs (they do not have to be on this season):

36. Name the film that you have seen most often in the past five years:

37. If you could see only one more film before you die, what would it be?

38. List any periodicals related to film that you have read in the past two months:

INSTRUCTIONS

Now you are going to see some films. We are interested in your predictions about what will happen next. At several intervals in each film the picture will black out for 15 seconds. Please check on the answer sheet, opposite the number corresponding to the number appearing on the screen, the responses that are closest to WHAT YOU THINK YOU WILL SEE IMMEDIATELY NEXT. (What you think you will actually see on the screen when the film resumes; not what you wish would happen or what you would do if you were making the film.)

You must make two choices each time the film stops. Pick one response in each of the two columns. (Note that the responses you choose from are the same for each break in the film.) For example:

GO ON TO THE NEXT PAGE

P-1 ____ this action continues   ____ same size
     ____ different action, same time   ____ tighter
     ____ different action, different time   ____ looser

The first column refers to the action of the last shot. If you think that it will continue, mark the first blank. If you think the scene will shift to different action (which you may have seen before, or which may be completely new) mark the second or the third blanks: the second, if you think that the action will be at the same time, or continuous in time, with the last shot; the third, if you think the action will take place in the past or the future (a lapse of time, a flash-back, or a flash-forward).

The second column refers to the size of the images in relation to the last shot. Mark the first blank if you predict no particular change; the second if you predict a tighter or closer shot; the third if you predict that the camera will pull back for a wider or looser shot.

Make one mark in each of the columns for each break in the film. If you don't know, guess. Respond to every question. Now we will see a short practice film; then you will have an opportunity to ask questions.

P-1 ____ this action continues   ____ same size
     ____ different action, same time   ____ tighter
     ____ different action, different time   ____ looser

P-2 ____ this action continues   ____ same size
     ____ different action, same time   ____ tighter
     ____ different action, different time   ____ looser

P-3 ____ this action continues   ____ same size
     ____ different action, same time   ____ tighter
     ____ different action, different time   ____ looser

CONTEMPORARY FILM RESEARCH I.D. _____112_____
217 Flint Hall   (same as on information sheet)
University of Kansas
Lawrence, Kansas 66044

The titles of a variety of films are listed below. Opposite each is a scale ranging from complete indifference to great excitation. Please respond on this scale to each film title, <u>whether or not you have seen the film</u>.

	completely indifferent				excites me greatly
Zorba the Greek	___	___	___	___	___
Rules of the Game	___	___	___	___	___
Time for Burning	___	___	___	___	___
Mash	___	___	___	___	___
Citizen Kane	___	___	___	___	___
Bonnie and Clyde	___	___	___	___	___
Hard Day's Night	___	___	___	___	___
Patton	___	___	___	___	___
Duck Soup	___	___	___	___	___
The Last Laugh	___	___	___	___	___
Casablanca	___	___	___	___	___
High School	___	___	___	___	___
Empire	___	___	___	___	___
Shane	___	___	___	___	___
The Sound of Music	___	___	___	___	___
Catch-22	___	___	___	___	___
Airport	___	___	___	___	___
Vertigo	___	___	___	___	___
Persona	___	___	___	___	___
Smart Aleck	___	___	___	___	___
Birth of a Nation	___	___	___	___	___
8½	___	___	___	___	___

CONTEMPORARY　　　　　　I.D. _____
FILM RESEARCH　　　　　　(same as on information sheet)

Now, for a change of pace, we would like to know what you think and feel about a number of important social and personal questions. The best answer to each statement below is your <u>personal opinion</u>. We have tried to cover many different and opposing points of view; you may find yourself agreeing strongly with some of the statements, disagreeing just as strongly with others, and perhaps uncertain about others; whether you agree or disagree with any statement, you can be sure many people feel the same as you do.

Mark each statement according to how much you agree or disagree with it. Please mark every one.

1. It is only natural that a person would have a much better acquaintance with the ideas he believes in than with ideas he opposes.

disagree	disagree	disagree	agree	agree	agree
very much	on the whole	a little	a little	on the whole	very much

4. I'd like it if I could find someone who would tell me how to solve my personal problems.

disagree	disagree	disagree	agree	agree	agree
very much	on the whole	a little	a little	on the whole	very much

6. In the history of mankind there have probably been just a handful of really great thinkers.

disagree	disagree	disagree	agree	agree	agree
very much	on the whole	a little	a little	on the whole	very much

7. In a heated discussion I generally become so absorbed in what I am going to say that I forget to listen to what the others are saying.

disagree	disagree	disagree	agree	agree	agree
very much	on the whole	a little	a little	on the whole	very much

8. If given the chance, I would do something of great benefit to the world.

disagree	disagree	disagree	agree	agree	agree
very much	on the whole	a little	a little	on the whole	very much

9. There are a number of people I have come to hate because of the things they stand for.

disagree	disagree	disagree	agree	agree	agree
very much	on the whole	a little	a little	on the whole	very much

10. It is only when a person devotes himself to an ideal or cause that life becomes meaningful.

disagree very much	disagree on the whole	disagree a little	agree a little	agree on the whole	agree very much
___	___	___	___	___	___

11. There are two kinds of people in this world: those who are for the truth and those who are against it.

disagree very much	disagree on the whole	disagree a little	agree a little	agree on the whole	agree very much
___	___	___	___	___	___

CONTEMPORARY FILM RESEARCH
217 Flint Hall
University of Kansas
Lawrence, Kansas 66044

PHOEBE   115

I.D. _____
(Same as on information sheet)
date _____

F-1 _____ this action continues   _____ same size
    _____ different action, same time   _____ tighter
    _____ different action, different time _____ looser

F-2 _____ this action continues   _____ same size
    _____ different action, same time   _____ tighter
    _____ different action, different time _____ looser

F-3 _____ this action continues   _____ same size
    _____ different action, same time   _____ tighter
    _____ different action, different time _____ looser

F-4 _____ this action continues   _____ same size
    _____ different action, same time   _____ tighter
    _____ different action, different time _____ looser

F-5 _____ this action continues   _____ same size
    _____ different action, same time   _____ tighter
    _____ different action, different time _____ looser

F-6 _____ this action continues   _____ same size
    _____ different action, same time   _____ tighter
    _____ different action, different time _____ looser

F-7 _____ this action continues   _____ same size
    _____ different action, same time   _____ tighter
    _____ different action, different time _____ looser

GO ON TO THE NEXT PAGE

PHOEBE 116

F-8 ____ this action continues   ____ same size
     ____ different action, same time   ____ tighter
     ____ different action, different time   ____ looser

F-9 ____ this action continues   ____ same size
     ____ different action, same time   ____ tighter
     ____ different action, different time   ____ looser

F-10 ____ this action continues   ____ same size
     ____ different action, same time   ____ tighter
     ____ different action, different time   ____ looser

F-11 ____ this action continues   ____ same size
     ____ different action, same time   ____ tighter
     ____ different action, different time   ____ looser

F-12 ____ this action continues   ____ same size
     ____ different action, same time   ____ tighter
     ____ different action, different time   ____ looser

F-13 ____ this action continues   ____ same size
     ____ different action, same time   ____ tighter
     ____ different action, different time   ____ looser

F-14 ____ this action continues   ____ same size
     ____ different action, same time   ____ tighter
     ____ different action, different time   ____ looser

F-15 ____ this action continues   ____ same size
     ____ different action, same time   ____ tighter
     ____ different action, different time   ____ looser

GO ON TO THE NEXT PAGE

PHOEBE 117

F-16 ____ this action continues   ____ same size
      ____ different action, same time   ____ tighter
      ____ different action, different time   ____ looser

F-17 ____ this action continues   ____ same size
      ____ different action, same time   ____ tighter
      ____ different action, different time   ____ looser

F-18 ____ this action continues   ____ same size
      ____ different action, same time   ____ tighter
      ____ different action, different time   ____ looser

F-19 ____ this action continues   ____ same size
      ____ different action, same time   ____ tighter
      ____ different action, different time   ____ looser

F-20 ____ this action continues   ____ same size
      ____ different action, same time   ____ tighter
      ____ different action, different time   ____ looser

F-21 ____ this action continues   ____ same size
      ____ different action, same time   ____ tighter
      ____ different action, different time   ____ looser

F-22 ____ this action continues   ____ same size
      ____ different action, same time   ____ tighter
      ____ different action, different time   ____ looser

F-23 ____ this action continues   ____ same size
      ____ different action, same time   ____ tighter
      ____ different action, different time   ____ looser

GO ON TO THE NEXT PAGE

PHOEBE 118

F-24 ____ this action continues   ____ same size

____ different action, same time   ____ tighter

____ different action, different time   ____ looser

F-25 ____ this action continues   ____ same size

____ different action, same time   ____ tighter

____ different action, different time   ____ looser

F-26 ____ this action continues   ____ same size

____ different action, same time   ____ tighter

____ different action, different time   ____ looser

Now, please, some feedback for us:

A. Have you ever seen this film, Phoebe, before? ____ 1. yes ____ 2. no

Please describe your feelings about this experience on the scales below:

B. ____   ____   ____   ____   ____
    boring   interesting

C. ____   ____   ____   ____   ____
    frustrating   satisfying

D. Indicate the confidence you felt that your predictions would be correct:

    ____   ____   ____   ____   ____
    no   very
    confidence   confident

E. As the film went on, did you get:

    ____   ____   ____   ____   ____
    less   more
    confident   confident

F. Please use the rest of this page for any comments you may have about this experience. Thank you.

CONTEMPORARY FILM RESEARCH
217 Flint Hall
University of Kansas
Lawrence, Kansas 66044

HOW DO I LOVE THEE [119]

I.D. _____
(same as on information sheet)
date: _____

K-1 ____ this action continues
    ____ different action, same time
    ____ different action, different time
    ____ same size
    ____ tighter
    ____ looser

K-2 ____ this action continues
    ____ different action, same time
    ____ different action, different time
    ____ same size
    ____ tighter
    ____ looser

K-3 ____ this action continues
    ____ different action, same time
    ____ different action, different time
    ____ same size
    ____ tighter
    ____ looser

K-4 ____ this action continues
    ____ different action, same time
    ____ different action, different time
    ____ same size
    ____ tighter
    ____ looser

K-5 ____ this action continues
    ____ different action, same time
    ____ different action, different time
    ____ same size
    ____ tighter
    ____ looser

K-6 ____ this action continues
    ____ different action, same time
    ____ different action, different time8
    ____ same size
    ____ tighter
    ____ looser

K-7 ____ this action continues
    ____ different action, same time
    ____ different action, different time
    ____ same size
    ____ tighter
    ____ looser

GO ON TO THE NEXT PAGE

HOW DO I LOVE THEE

K-8 ____ this action continues   ____ same size
     ____ different action, same time   ____ tighter
     ____ different action, different time   ____ looser

K-9 ____ this action continues   ____ same size
     ____ different action, same time   ____ tighter
     ____ different action, different time   ____ looser

K-10 ____ this action continues   ____ same size
     ____ different action, same time   ____ tighter
     ____ different action, different time   ____ looser

L-1 ____ this action continues   ____ same size
     ____ different action, same time   ____ tighter
     ____ different action, different time   ____ looser

L-2 ____ this action continues   ____ same size
     ____ different action, same time   ____ tighter
     ____ different action, different time   ____ looser

L-3 ____ this action continues   ____ same size
     ____ different action, same time   ____ tighter
     ____ different action, different time   ____ looser

L-4 ____ this action continues   ____ same size
     ____ different action, same time   ____ tighter
     ____ different action, different time   ____ looser

L-5 ____ this action continues   ____ same size
     ____ different action, same time   ____ tighter
     ____ different action, different time   ____ looser

GO ON TO THE NEXT PAGE

HOW DO I LOVE THEE 121

L-6 ____ this action continues   ____ same size
     ____ different action, same time   ____ tighter
     ____ different action, different time   ____ looser

L-7 ____ this action continues   ____ same size
     ____ different action, same time   ____ tighter
     ____ different action, different time   ____ looser

L-8 ____ this action continues   ____ same size
     ____ different action, same time   ____ tighter
     ____ different action, different time   ____ looser

L-9 ____ this action continues   ____ same size
     ____ different action, same time   ____ tighter
     ____ different action, different time   ____ looser

L-10 ____ this action continues   ____ same size
     ____ different action, same time   ____ tighter
     ____ different action, different time   ____ looser

L-11 ____ this action continues   ____ same size
     ____ different action, same time   ____ tighter
     ____ different action, different time   ____ looser

L-12 ____ this action continues   ____ same size
     ____ different action, same time   ____ tighter
     ____ different action, different time   ____ looser

G-8 ____ this action continues   ____ same size
     ____ different action, same time   ____ tighter
     ____ different action, different time   ____ looser

GO ON TO THE NEXT PAGE

HOW DO I LOVE THEE 122

G-9   ____ this action continues   ____ same size
      ____ different action, same time   ____ tighter
      ____ different action, different time ____ looser

G-10 ____ this action continues   ____ same size
      ____ different action, same time   ____ tighter
      ____ different action, different time ____ looser

F-30 ____ this action continues   ____ same size
      ____ different action, same time   ____ tighter
      ____ different action, different time ____ looser

Now, please, some feedback for us:

A. Have you seen this film, How Do I Love Thee, before? ____ 1. yes ____ 2. no

Please describe your feelings about this experience on the scales below:

B. ____   ____   ____   ____   ____
    boring   interesting

C. ____   ____   ____   ____   ____
    frustrating   satisfying

D. Indicate the confidence you felt that your predictions would be correct:

    ____   ____   ____   ____   ____
    no   very
    confidence   confident

E. As the film went on, did you get:

    ____   ____   ____   ____   ____
    less   more
    confident   confident

F. Please use the rest of this page for any comments you may have about this experience. Thank you.

APPENDIX D

SAMPLE OF RESULTS

FROM MAIN TEST

RESPONSE FREQUENCIES, PHOEBE, PLOT LEVEL

		Sophisticated			Naive		
Foil Numbers		1	2	3	1	2	3
Item	Correct Foil	this action continues	different action same time	different action different time	this action continues	different action same time	different action different time
1	1	15	4	0	45	11	2
2	1	6	7	6	16	22	20
3	2	11	7	1	36	17	5
4	3	15	2	2	41	10	7
5	1	9	2	8	23	7	28
6	1	4	8	7	11	23	24
7	1	13	2	4	38	8	12
8	3	12	0	7	34	4	19
9	1	5	10	4	19	19	20
10	1	9	9	1	32	21	5
11	3	1	7	11	9	18	31
12	1	16	2	1	42	6	10
13	3	7	2	10	45	4	9
14	3	5	0	14	20	7	31
15	3	1	1	17	5	10	43
16	3	1	2	16	17	11	30
17	1	4	6	9	21	17	20
18	2	8	7	4	21	26	11
19	3	5	1	12	26	12	20
20	3	1	1	16	17	3	38
21	2	5	2	11	28	8	22
22	3	9	1	9	34	3	21
23	3	0	0	19	7	9	42
24	3	10	3	6	17	20	21
25	1	10	1	8	34	5	19
26	1	7	3	9	11	11	35

RESPONSE FREQUENCIES, PHOEBE, SHOT LEVEL

		Sophisticated			Naive		
		same size	tighter	looser	same size	tighter	looser
Foil Numbers		1	2	3	1	2	3
Item	Correct Foil						
1	1	10	7	2	30	18	10
2	3	1	1	17	6	3	49
3	1	6	4	9	31	14	13
4	2	1	18	0	6	50	2
5	1	1	18	0	14	41	3
6	3	6	10	3	18	29	11
7	2	4	15	0	18	40	0
8	2	3	16	0	10	45	3
9	3	10	3	6	28	16	14
10	1	1	3	15	12	10	36
11	3	5	1	13	7	7	44
12	3	8	8	3	38	10	10
13	1	9	5	5	26	27	5
14	3	4	2	13	18	13	27
15	3	2	2	15	15	4	39
16	2	8	8	3	39	8	11
17	2	3	7	9	31	9	18
18	3	0	0	19	11	4	43
19	3	9	0	9	25	11	22
20	3	2	0	16	25	9	24
21	3	7	1	10	28	8	22
22	3	9	9	1	25	26	7
23	2	2	17	0	10	45	3
24	3	9	4	6	29	8	21
25	1	5	13	1	23	35	0
26	2	6	9	4	29	11	17

RESPONSE FREQUENCIES, LOVE THEE, PLOT LEVEL

		Sophisticated			Naive		
Foil Numbers		1	2	3	1	2	3
Item	Correct Foil	this action continues	different action same time	different action different time	this action continues	different action same time	different action different time
1	1	19	5	0	60	5	0
2	1	23	1	0	59	5	1
3	2	9	4	11	14	24	7
4	1	11	10	3	27	22	16
5	1	23	0	1	60	5	0
6	2	0	0	24	0	1	64
7	1	18	5	1	50	11	4
8	1	12	5	7	29	19	17
9	3	6	0	18	21	12	32
10	1	15	2	7	33	13	19
11	1	23	1	0	53	4	8
12	1	13	1	10	29	14	21
13	1	23	1	0	61	4	0
14	1	16	2	6	32	15	18
15	1	24	0	0	60	3	2
16	3	1	0	23	0	8	57
17	1	24	0	0	64	0	1
18	1	22	2	0	57	5	3
19	1	7	7	10	10	31	24
20	3	6	2	16	28	16	21
21	1	24	0	0	64	1	0
22	3	5	2	17	11	7	47
23	1	22	1	1	53	7	5
24	3	4	2	18	5	10	50
25	1	24	0	0	62	2	0
26	1	24	0	0	59	2	3

RESPONSE FREQUENCIES, LOVE THEE, SHOT LEVEL

		Sophisticated			Naive		
		same size	tighter	looser	same size	tighter	looser
Foil Numbers		1	2	3	1	2	3
Item	Correct Foil						
1	2	13	10	1	47	18	0
2	1	17	0	7	41	4	20
3	3	4	2	18	18	9	38
4	2	8	3	13	21	10	34
5	3	18	4	2	30	13	22
6	3	2	0	22	4	1	60
7	2	4	15	5	28	25	12
8	3	14	1	9	32	9	24
9	3	5	1	18	14	5	46
10	1	11	4	9	23	14	28
11	1	13	9	2	41	15	9
12	3	4	2	18	16	0	48
13	1	14	3	7	31	22	12
14	1	7	3	14	31	4	30
15	2	11	13	0	36	26	3
16	3	2	0	22	4	2	59
17	1	21	3	0	45	19	1
18	1	16	1	7	38	6	21
19	2	2	17	5	8	47	10
20	1	15	4	5	34	14	17
21	2	8	15	1	28	37	0
22	3	4	1	19	11	5	49
23	3	14	7	3	40	12	13
24	1	12	3	9	35	8	22
25	1	6	17	1	26	37	1
26	1	17	0	7	39	16	9

DISSERTATIONS ON FILM

An Arno Press Collection

Anderson, Patrick Donald. **In Its Own Image:** The Cinematic Vision of Hollywood. First publication, 1978

Bacher, Lutz. **The Mobile Mise En Scene:** A Critical Analysis of the Theory and Practice of Long-Take Camera Movement in the Narrative Film. First publication, 1978

Beaver, Frank Eugene. **Bosley Crowther:** Social Critic of the Film, 1940-1967. First publication, 1974

Benderson, Albert Edward. **Critical Approaches to Federico Fellini's "8½".** First publication, 1974

Berg, Charles Merrell. **An Investigation of the Motives for and Realization of Music to Accompany the American Silent Film, 1896-1927. First publication, 1976**

Blades, Joseph Dalton, Jr. **A Comparative Study of Selected American Film Critics, 1958-1974.** First publication, 1976

Blake, Richard Aloysius. **The Lutheran Milieu of the Films of Ingmar Bergman.** First publication, 1978

Bohn, Thomas William. **An Historical and Descriptive Analysis of the "Why We Fight" Series.** First publication, 1977

Cohen, Louis Harris. **The Cultural-Political Traditions and Developments of the Soviet Cinema: 1917-1972.** First publication, 1974

Dart, Peter. **Pudovkin's Films and Film Theory.** First publication, 1974

Davis, Robert Edward. **Response to Innovation:** A Study of Popular Argument about New Mass Media. First publication, 1976

Facey, Paul W. **The Legion of Decency:** A Sociological Analysis of the Emergence and Development of a Social Pressure Group. First publication, 1974

Feineman, Neil. **Persistence of Vision:** The Films of Robert Altman. First publication, 1978

Feldman, Charles Matthew. **The National Board of Censorship (Review) of Motion Pictures, 1909-1922.** First publication, 1977

Feldman, Seth R. **Evolution of Style in the Early Work of Dziga Vertov.** First publication, 1977

Flanders, Mark Wilson. **Film Theory of James Agee.** First publication, 1977

Fredericksen, Donald Laurence. **The Aesthetic of Isolation in Film Theory:** Hugo Munsterberg. First publication, 1977

Gosser, H. Mark. **Selected Attempts at Stereoscopic Moving Pictures and Their Relationship to the Development of Motion Picture Technology, 1852-1903.** First publication, 1977

Harpole, Charles Henry. **Gradients of Depth in the Cinema Image.** First publication, 1978

James, C. Rodney. **Film as a National Art:** NFB of Canada and the Film Board Idea. First publication, 1977

Karimi, A.M. **Toward a Definition of the American Film Noir (1941-1949).** First publication, 1976

Karpf, Stephen L. **The Gangster Film:** Emergence, Variation and Decay of a Genre, 1930-1940. First publication, 1973

Lounsbury, Myron O. **The Origins of American Film Criticism, 1909-1939.** First publication, 1973

Lynch, F. Dennis. **Clozentropy:** A Technique for Studying Audience Response to Films. First publication, 1978

Lyons, Robert J[oseph]. **Michelangelo Antonioni's Neo-Realism:** A World View. First publication, 1976

Lyons, Timothy James. **The Silent Partner:** The History of the American Film Manufacturing Company, 1910-1921. First publication, 1974

McLaughlin, Robert. **Broadway and Hollywood:** A History of Economic Interaction. First publication, 1974

Maland, Charles J. **American Visions:** The Films of Chaplin, Ford, Capra, and Welles, 1936-1941. First publication, 1977

Mason, John L. **The Identity Crisis Theme in American Feature Films, 1960-1969.** First publication, 1977

North, Joseph H. **The Early Development of the Motion Picture, 1887-1909.** First publication, 1973

Paine, Jeffery Morton. **The Simplification of American Life:** Hollywood Films of the 1930's. First publication, 1977

Pryluck, Calvin. **Sources of Meaning in Motion Pictures and Television.** First publication, 1976

Rimberg, John. **The Motion Picture in the Soviet Union, 1918-1952.** First publication, 1973

Sanderson, Richard Arlo. **A Historical Study of the Development of American Motion Picture Content and Techniques Prior to 1904.** First publication, 1977

Sands, Pierre N. **A Historical Study of the Academy of the Motion Picture Arts and Sciences (1927-1947).** First publication, 1973

Selby, Stuart Alan. **The Study of Film as an Art Form in American Secondary Schools.** First publication, 1978

Shain, Russell Earl. **An Analysis of Motion Pictures about War Released by the American Film Industry, 1939-1970.** First publication, 1976

Snyder, John J. **James Agee:** A Study of His Film Criticism. First publication, 1977

Stuart, Frederic. **The Effects of Television on the Motion Picture and Radio Industries.** First publication, 1976

Van Wert, William F. **The Theory and Practice of the** *Ciné-Roman.* First publication, 1978

Wead, George. **Buster Keaton and the Dynamics of Visual Wit.** First publication, 1976

Welsch, Janice R. **Film Archetypes:** Sisters, Mistresses, Mothers and Daughters. First publication, 1978

Wolfe, Glenn J. **Vachel Lindsay:** The Poet as Film Theorist. First publication, 1973

Zuker, Joel Stewart. **Ralph Steiner:** Filmmaker and Still Photographer. First publication, 1978

DATE DUE

GAYLORD			PRINTED IN U.S.A.